FRONTIERS OF THE AFTERLIFE

FRONTIERS OF THE AFTERLIFE

EDWARD C. RANDALL

Frontiers of the Afterlife

This edition published in Great Britain in 2010 by
White Crow Books

White Crow Books is an imprint of
White Crow Productions Ltd
PO Box 1013
Guildford
GU1 9EJ

www.whitecrowbooks.com

Text design and eBook production by Essential Works
www.essentialworks.co.uk

Hardback ISBN 978-1-907661-34-1
Paperback ISBN 978-1-907355-30-1
eBook ISBN 978-1-907355-63-9

Religion & Spirituality

Distributed in the UK by
Lightning Source Ltd.
Chapter House
Pitfield
Kiln Farm
Milton Keynes MK11 3LW

Distributed in the USA by
Lightning Source Inc.
246 Heil Quaker Boulevard
LaVergne
Tennessee 37086

Contents

Foreword

SEPTEMBER IN THE north land! Nature has not been prodigal with her colors this Autumn; the frosts came early, so the forests change slowly; but yesterday, as if by magic, there was gold among the green, and today there is purple and red; hilltops blaze with their crowns of maple, slopes show grey in the sunlight, vines straggle here and there in lines of bronze, and the great timber reaches stand out in their somber shades.

Again I have crossed the Canadian border and come into the heart of the wilderness, into the silence where one can think deeply. Here in a cabin, where I have spent many summers, there is a quiet not to be found in the great cities. The crisp air, clean and pure, stimulates like old wine, and the moving waters along the wooded shores soothe tired nerves.

It is good at times to be alone – alone in the heart of a great forest. Listening, one hears new sounds, new voices, voices of the woodland, voices of the furtive folk, voices of the swaying trees and moving waters, voices everywhere – for wherever there is life there is language, language of which we in our wisdom get only an indefinite impression. I have heard other voices – voices of those the world calls dead – on more than seven hundred nights, covering a period of twenty-two years, aided by a wonderful psychic, I talked with those in the afterlife, they using their own vocal organs just as I did.

This astounding statement, owing to lack of knowledge and to erroneous conceptions, staggers the ordinary imagination. These facts will not be grasped, without explaining how it is done and describing the conditions which make speech with spirit people possible. I am going to tell, if I can, in language that may be understood, what the great change actually is and to what it leads. In order to do this, the first fact that must be brought home is that here and now our real body is our inner body; that what is visible and tangible is the flesh garment, which we wear while an inhabitant of this plane; that dissolution is only a separation – a severance of the inner body from the flesh garment; that both are material and that thereafter the spirit body is identically the same as before – the same, but lacking the outer covering.

Also, the place inhabited by all these so called dead is as material and tangible as this earth, and, given the right conditions, those who have gone from us can talk voice to voice with us as when in earthly life.

How stupendous the undertaking! Notwithstanding the great privilege that has been mine, greater perhaps than that enjoyed by most people, I feel unequal to the task, and were it not for the consciousness that an invisible group would in some way guide and help, I question my courage.

All this cannot be done by mere statement of conclusions. Such is human mentality, that each condition must be illustrated and explained, the principle involved must be expounded and made to appeal to one's reason; otherwise, it goes for naught. I have, in many cases, left the explanation of these great problems in the actual words of those who now live over the border; I have quoted their statements, describing dissolution, the place where they live and what they do to sustain and enrich themselves in their life from day to day. I will also let them tell something of the effect in that plane of acts and thoughts on this one.

In order to think clearly, I find I must be far from the confusion of business, in harmony with nature, in tune with natural vibrations. For that reason, and to fulfill a promise made to a group of spirit people, I have sought the seclusion of this forest home, as I have done before, to tell again to a hungry world something of what I have learned of the conditions following so-called death.

The twilight gathers; the day and night are blending; purple shadows in the west; the great logs crack; the fire warms; the winds sigh in the branches; and over the wooded island across the bay the full moon glints and rises majestically in the concave sky, flooding the world with light and making a pathway to my cabin door.

The problem of life and death is the most vital of all that confront mankind, and the least understood. Here in the quiet of this place all the so-called dead come close. Though I possess no psychic sight or hearing, such has been my speech and acquaintance with them, that they come at the thought call and hold mental speech with me. I catch their silent suggestion.

Death is unknown in nature. Change comes to the human race and man is changing day by day, but final dissolution is only another step in his progression.

Those that have gone since the earth was first populated live on, and we who tread the earth today will live on. They now hold speech with those who still inhabit the earth plane, as we may do when we join them, if conditions are right. And as communication is better perfected, there will be a better understanding, and finer development, as we come to know this law.

The past comes to me like a dream. Again I hear the voices of those who have gone before, speaking words of encouragement and words of wisdom. I feel again the touch of their hands vibrating beyond measure, yet warm and natural for the moment. And their faces, clothed for an instant with material as when they lived here, I see now in memory as when I saw in fact.

Dissolution will mean little to me, for I know something of the reality of the afterlife and I have, in my years of work, made many friends there. I will not go as a stranger to a strange land, but as one who has, by effort, gained some knowledge of conditions to be met, and many of those who reside there, whom I never knew in the physical body, I shall have the privilege of calling my friends.

How astounding the fact that human life is lived with no thought of the morrow, with little or no regard of what waits beyond!

Nature has a purpose in all things. What is man's purpose? We come out of the invisible, stay for a little time, and go back to the invisible; but which is the real? How many ever give this subject the slightest consideration? What is man's conception of it, and how must he live and what must he do, to meet with self-respect the life beyond?

The morning breaks. I go out on the broad veranda and face the east, as the September sun shows above the hills. It has shown millions of times before and will shine when all that now live in this physical plane are forgotten, and when new generations have taken their place and property. I see about me in volcanic rock, in fossil fragments stolen from decay, in valleys worn between the hills, in ridges lifted from the underworld, in various forms of life, the record of earth's countless ages. In retrospection, I see the bursting bud and leaf and flower in the spring, the fullness and glory of the summer, and the golden autumn, emblematic of man's birth, growth and passing. Just a short season and the twilight will fall upon the past, our physical eyes will dim, the mind fail to record the memory of events, our ears will become dull, the pulse pause, brain lose the power to think, then, as quietly as the dawn meets morning, the separation comes. Out of the housing of the flesh, the inner material body emerges, though we see it not, and it is welcomed by those who have gone before. This is the second birth, so like the first, except that all the knowledge, individuality and spirituality gained in our earth life is retained, and we as a people live on in the fullness of our mentality and strength as before.

Dissolution neither adds to nor subtracts from the sum total of our knowledge. The inner material body in which we have functioned, we shall still function in for all eternity. This is what I am endeavoring to explain as it has been told to me. Such is the incentive to write this book.

EDWARD C. RANDALL, BUFFALO, NY 1922

1

The Great Question

SINCE MANKIND CAME up out of savagery, the great problem has been: What is the ultimate end? What, if anything, awaits on the other side of death's mysterious door? What happens when the hour strikes that closes man's earth career, when, leaving all the gathered wealth of lands and goods, he goes out into the dark alone? Is death the end – annihilation and repose? Or, does he wake in some other sphere or condition, retaining personality?

Each must solve this great question for himself. Dissolution and change have come to every form of life, and will come to all that live. With opportunity knocking at the door, mankind has but little more appreciation of it now than it had when Phallic-worship swayed the destinies of empires. It may be that, as a people, our development has been such that we could heretofore grasp and comprehend only length, breadth, and thickness, the three accepted physical dimensions of matter; that in our progression we have but now become able to appreciate and understand life beyond the physical plane.

Time was when all knowledge was handed down from one generation to another by story, song and tradition. When the Persian civilization was growing old and ambition towered above the lofty walls of Babylon; when Egypt was building her temples on the banks of the Nile; when Greece was the center of art and culture, and Rome with its wealth and luxuries held sway over the civilized world, they were not ready for, and could not appreciate, that progress which has come. The world cannot stand still. The great law of the universe is progress. Two or three generations since, the idea that a cable would one day be laid under the sea and the messages would be transmitted under the waters from continent to continent, was laughed at as a chimera. Only a little while ago, the world could not comprehend that words and sentences could be flashed across the trackless ocean from ship to ship, and from land to land, without wires.

And who shall now say that it is not possible to send thoughts, words, sentences, voices even, and messages, out into the ether of the spirit world, there to be heard, recorded and answered? Has man reached the end of his possibilities; will all progression stop with Marconi's achievements?

This is the age of man; we have passed the age of the gods. If our development is such that we can comprehend the life and the conditions following dissolution, it must be within our grasp as surely as progress has been possible at all times and among all people since the world began.

Assuming, then, that we have come to that period, when we can look upon all subjects and propositions impartially and intelligently, no longer bound by fear, past or present, we can now appreciate that it is of the greatest importance to know what follows this life.

We are swinging away from the old moorings; new views come with changing times and conditions. Knowledge is the torch that fires our enthusiasm and makes advancement possible. It is not the past, but the future, that commands our attention. We may learn much of nature as she speaks, in all dialects, her various tongues. All truth is safe, nothing else will suffice, and he who holds back the truth, through expediency or fear, fails in his duty to mankind.

Our age is one of sudden and rapid changes; the people are in a state of transition. Most minds are sensitive, alert and versatile. It is a period fraught with unrest and thirst for knowledge. What was true yesterday, assumes a different, one could almost say a diametrically opposite, aspect today. This is a period fruitful in scientific discoveries, and in the adaptation of the universal law of vibratory action. Much that is said now could not have been explained twenty years ago. Mankind has progressed to that point where it can comprehend life as it exists in the great beyond, and, as surely as day follows the night, he will come to understand it. That force which directs the destiny of all living things, seems to have planned it for this time, and many, like myself, are but instruments directed by that great force that we call Good and others call God.

Many have come to know what awaits over the great divide, have solved the great problem of dissolution, and, with the confidence born of knowledge, based on facts proved and demonstrated, speak with authority.

The thought that there need be no more groping in the dark makes the pulse quicken. The realization that fear can now be eliminated from the human brain fills every heart with joy. The fact that we may come into touch with those in spheres beyond and know that they live, and how and where they live, will lift the burden of sorrow from every heart that mourns its dead.

We of older growth are but children in the wilderness of these new and subtle laws. Before we can grasp and comprehend this philosophy we must eliminate false conceptions and erroneous ideas, and come to the subject with open mind. That this is a difficult task I well know, for minds filled with traditions and false or no conceptions of the afterlife, simply cannot at once comprehend the truth when it is given to them. There can be no individual progression until one becomes free, mentally poised, open to reason and willing to hear facts and to weigh them honestly. The blind are entitled to our sympathy; we look, with sorrow, upon those who cannot accept a truth, because it is not as they have been taught; but we grasp the open hand of the free, walk with them along nature's highway, and reason together.

Man, in his ignorance, is like the bewildered stream blindly groping its way down the steep hillside, turned in its course by every resistance it meets; rushing, retreating and halting, moved by the weak force of an inferior instinct. Some invisible power carries it onward. It little knows the nature of that power. It seems to be carried by an impulse from within. After a time the stream grows wider and deeper, its current less swift. Then it enlarges to the calm, peaceful river which flows steadily and unerringly through the wide valleys on its appointed way to the sea. Likewise, man is led onward by the mysterious force of a superior destiny. At first he rushes about impetuously, and murmurs because of the restrictions imposed by the law. But his consciousness grows broader and deeper with the march of the years, and in the clear waters of mind he sees a reflection of some of the great truths of the universe. His visions of the beauty of that inner world of ideas inspire him to a life of noble endeavor.

Humanity, as a whole, is like the streams and rivers of earth. All men are moving irresistibly onward, carried by some mysterious power they feel, but cannot fathom. Humanity at last will reach the boundless sea, where there will be no discord, no unrealized yearnings, no limitation. Deep down in the still waters all hearts will find peace.

Humanity is awakening. The mind has, at last, become active, and now demands to know what fate awaits us beyond the grave. Man has learned something about himself and the universe, and this knowledge is making him free. This is an age of intellectual emancipation. Those who walk with open eyes will find the truth, for it lights the way across the continent of every human life.

2

The Inner Spirit Body

"THERE IS A NATURAL body, and there is a spiritual body." Those words have fallen from the lips of priests, over the bodies of the so-called dead, for thousands of years, yet not a single minister who uttered them, nor one among the millions of mourners, who for centuries past heard them, ever formed any rational conception of what they meant and for ages the world has been filled with sorrow.

Had they understood nature's purpose, and known the advantages which the so-called dead gained through the process of dissolution, they would have been comforted. In the presence of such truth, all creeds wither and decay, and old teachings fail to satisfy. That this is a fact, every one who mourns must testify. There must be something wrong with a system of philosophy or a teaching that always fails when put to the test. When the earth clods fall upon the physical body of one held dear, hope sees a star; but hope is not knowledge, and tears fall on furrowed cheeks. If those who still remain but knew that death, as it is called, was only change – a progression – and that the departed still live, and if they knew about their present abiding place, the world of gloom would turn to one of joy.

There is a natural, by that I mean a physical, body, and there is a spiritual body; but those bare propositions, standing alone, convey nothing to the human mind. They must be followed by facts explaining, if it be a fact, how there can possibly be two bodies in one when only one is visible to sight and sensible to touch. Without knowing the law of nature involved, without proof that one survives, although the other goes back to mingle with the elements from whence it came, it is utterly impossible to comprehend what was intended by the words first quoted.

I have seen spirit bodies materialize, have touched them and found them as the natural. I have heard them speak and tell over and over again that they had bodies, the same bodies as when they lived the earth life. Still I was not satisfied, and sought to know the character of the two, how they blended, how they worked as one, what natural law was involved, what happened in the dissolution process, why two were necessary, to the end that I might comprehend the fact, for until such knowledge was acquired I had only a very hazy idea, if any, of the situation.

As fast as I was able to comprehend the facts, they were given me, and lo and behold, like all natural laws, I found all simple.

This planet is but one in the federation of the infinite. All the universe is filled with life, and on this earth, as on others, this force impregnates, finds lodgment, and is clothed in physical garments, to the end that it may increase, multiply, develop, and in time go back to the infinite from whence it came. In that manner and through that process, it increases the sum total of what we call God or universal good, but it is only by change that that process designed by the Infinite can be carried forward, and death, so-called, is but one of the steps in life's progression.

When matter is receptive, an atom from the life

mass is clothed, and from the moment of conception commences its journey back to its source. How fast it develops, what progress it makes, depends much on environment. Its form depends upon the substance which clothes it. Whether physical expression appears as man or animal, in earth, rocks, growing things or the water of the sea, depends on how, and under what conditions, it obtains its start here. All is life, expressed in visible form, and where there is life there is thought, and neither life nor thought can be destroyed.

There is also physical evidence tending to prove the same proposition. One has his leg amputated, and still feels that he can move his foot; another loses his arm, but still can use his hand and move his fingers. Such is their impression and feeling. Many with whom I have talked are very serious in this matter, and they are right – amputation can only remove the covering of an arm or leg; no part of the etheric body form can be cut off. This remains intact, whatever occurs to the outer covering, for in dissolution it appears intact. A body in that advanced plane may be undeveloped, shrunken and deformed, but it will be all there, and it will appear just as one has made it.

Life is expressed in form; without form it could not function. We cannot see the mighty oak in the heart of the acorn, but it is there in all its splendid promise. We cannot see man, the wonder of creation, in the fluid that first clothes it in its conception, but man is there with form and feature, strength and character, which will ever have continuity. With mankind the spirit body is clothed, in the beginning, with a flesh garment, a material vibrating more slowly than the ether of which it is composed, and the process of growth commences.

The next change is the physical birth; then comes earth life and the development, physical and spiritual; next is the separation of the spiritual from the outer covering in the change called death – no more wonderful and not half so mysterious as birth; then on, to climb the heights in everlasting life. Such are the teachings that have come to me, voice to voice, from spirit people – some whom I personally have known, and others whom I have come to know and respect in this work.

Volumes could be written on this subject from what is now known. Every man, woman and child living on this earth plane, did possess in the beginning, and possesses now, an inner or spirit body, composed and made up of that material we call ether, a substance and material so fine and of such rapid vibration that the physical eye can not see it. This inner or etheric body alone has sensation. It takes form and feature, stature and expression, while earth life lasts, and retains these in the next life as well.

This inner spirit body, during this stage of its development, is simply clothed, covered or housed in a visible, slowly vibrating garment that we call flesh, which has no sensation. This is evident from the fact that when the one is separated from the other, the outer body has no sensation or motion, so that it decays and loses form.

That experience called death is nature's process by which the two are separated. The habitation, for some cause, becomes unfit for further occupancy. The spirit, or the inner body, is released for further progression from the tenement which is no longer habitable. The earth body goes back into its elements, to be used again to clothe other forms of life. The inner or spirit body, holding its same form, invisible then as before, but functioning as before, labors and finds further opportunity for growth and spirituality. This it finds in the zones or belts that surround this globe, and, when proper conditions are made, it answers to our call, and tells us of life in its new plane, invisible to mortal eye.

I asked this question of Dr. David Hossack, who has been in spirit life nearly a century:

"Is my understanding correct, that here and now we have, and possess, an inner etheric body, which, divested of its flesh garment, passes intact to the spirit world?"

In reply he said: "There is an inner, etheric body, composed of minute particles, of such substance that it can, and does, pass into spirit life. Your outer bodies are too gross and material to effect the change. The inner body is but the mind, the thought, the soul of the person. It is in the semblance of the material body, but whether beautiful or ugly, strong or weak, depends upon the inner life of the person to whom belongs that particular spark of the great radiance called life, or God.

"Some there be who build a fair body, and some there be who come into this life with a body so misshapen and sickly it takes much effort to effect an upright, clean one. They all come with bodies naturally, as all things have minds, after one fashion or another; but the conditions of these bodies are very different. Naturally, the mind, being the reality of man, is that which lives on, beautiful or disfigured by good or evil thoughts, as the case may be. The only comfort is that every one has opportunity here to work out the change in himself, and sometimes those changes are very rapid."

Another said:

"In earth life I gave all for wearing apparel; and when I reached the spirit world, I did not have rags enough to cover me, and the beauty of my form had vanished. I was misshapen and distorted. At first I could not understand that it was my spiritual body that was so deformed, for I had not given the spiritual part of me a thought while on earth. In fact, the earth was all in all for me, and I did not trouble myself to think of another life, deeming the time better spent in enjoying the things I knew I possessed.

"A spirit came and offered to clothe me, but no sooner did the garments touch my body than they were discolored. My progress has been slow, but after many years of suffering I have developed my spirit and restored its beauty, but it is different from what it was in the life below:"

But evidence of all things spiritual must, of necessity, come from those who live there. Their condition is different, their laws are different, for they live in a world invisible to our eyes, and we cannot insist, if we would understand their life, on applying physical laws and methods. It is from spirit people that I have sought knowledge, and from them, and through years of investigation and research, I have come to know as a fact that "there is a natural body and there is a spiritual body."

3

The Death Change

WHAT HAPPENS AT DEATH? What are one's sensations, and what meets the vision on awakening? This has been described thousands of times, and I quote from my records something of what I have been told on the important subject: "It is a privilege to tell you of my transition. The last physical sensation that I recall was one of falling, but I had no fear – it seemed so natural. At the same time I heard voices speaking words of encouragement, voices that I recognized as those of loved ones that I thought dead. For a time I had no recollection. Then I awoke in this spirit sphere, and never will I forget the joy that was mine. I found myself; saw my body, which appeared as usual, except lighter and more ethereal. I was resting on a couch in a beautiful room filled with flowers. I looked through a window and saw the landscape, bathed in rose-colored light. There was a quiet that was impressive, then music, the harmonious vibration of which seemed to rise and fall softly. Then one appeared, and, though she spoke no words, I seemed to understand and answered.

"In this thought language she told me that she had been my guardian while in the old body, and now that I had been released she would take me over the home that I had in my life been building.

She said: "This room so beautiful is the result of your self-denial and the happiness you brought to others, but there are others not so pleasing; and we passed into another that was dark and filled with rubbish; the air was heavy. This, my guide said, was built through my selfishness. Then to another, a little better lighted. I was told that every effort to do better created something brighter. Then into the garden where, among beautiful flowers, grew obnoxious weeds, the result of spiritual idleness.

"The house must all be made beautiful," she said, the weeds of idleness uprooted; and this can only be done by yourself, through work in the lower planes, by helping others."

My father's experience he described to me as follows: "You will recall the day of my dissolution. I had been in poor health for some months. That morning the air was so soft and warm, and the sun so bright, I wanted to be out in it, so I took my horse and buggy and started for a village about seven miles distant. As I drove along, a weakness seemed to come upon me and I partially reclined on the seat. Even then, though seventy-six years of age, I had no thought that my passing was near. As I arrived at the house where I was going, the sensation of weakness increased, but I was able to walk in unaided and sat in a chair. The faintness increased, and, raising my eyes, I saw your mother standing in the room, smiling. Startled, I arose to my feet, and my last earthly sensation was falling – and, as I now know, I did pitch forward on my face. I do not recall striking the floor, or pain in my death change. When the separation came, I was like one in sleep.

"The next I recall was awaking in the same room, with the leader of your spirit group holding my hand, helping me up. I had heard his wonderful voice many times when I was privileged to come into your work, but it took me some little time to realize what happened to me. I saw my body on the floor. This startled me, for the body I then had was to my sight and touch identical with the one lying so quiet. I saw people hurrying, and heard the anxious talk, not yet comprehending my separation from the physical body.

"I turned to your old friend, and mine, and asked him what had happened. He answered:

"Have you not been told when you talked with us in your son's home, that death was the separation of the inner from the outward body?"

"I recall that statement," I replied, "but I never comprehended it."

"You have just made that change," he said; you are now an inhabitant of the spirit world and one of us."

"I was deeply impressed with what he said, but dazed. I could not realize that the something called death was behind me, and that in me there had been no change, for I was the same in appearance and thought as before. Then memory quickened, and I commenced to think of what it meant. I could not think clearly, and my guide said, "Come with me for a little time and rest, and all will be well with you." I went with him, and those I saw and what I was I will tell you another time."

"This is another's description:

I remember seeing about me those that had been dead for a long time. This impressed me greatly, but I did not realize it fully. Then I felt a peculiar sensation all through my body. Then I seemed to rise up out of my body and come down quietly on the floor.

"I was in the same room, but there seemed to be two of me, one on the bed and one beside the bed. All about were my family in deep grief, why I could not tell, for my great pain was gone and I felt much better. Some of those whom I recognized as persons who had died, asked me to go, and with that thought I was outside and apparently could walk on the air. My next thought was that it was a dream and that I would awake and feel again the terrible pain. I was gently told what had happened, and I felt that God had been unjust to take me when I had so much to do, and when I was so needed by my family. I was not satisfied with the place I was in. About me there was a fog, and I started to walk out of it, but the farther I walked, the more dense it got, and I became discouraged and sat down by the wayside in deep grief. I had ever tried to provide the very best for those dependent on me. Where was my reward? Then someone approached, came as it were out of the fog, and I told him of my life work and complained of the condition I was in, and questioned the justice of it. He replied, "Yours was a selfish love; you worked for self. You should have made others happy as well as your own." He promised to help me in my great trouble, if I would help myself. Together we have worked, and now all is well; it is light and glorious. But that first awakening was not all that could be desired. My greatest disappointment after my awakening was when I returned to my old home, for I discovered that none could see or feel me, and all grieved for me as one dead, and their sorrow held me. I wept with them, and could not get away, until time healed their sorrow:

"How terrible it is that the world that has made so much progress in many things knows little of this greatest change, and the little it does know has almost been forced upon it by a few that know this truth and have the courage to stand for it.

These descriptions, as I review what I have written, do not give a fair idea of an average death change, and looking through my records I find another more normal:

"I left the physical world rich. I had little money, but day by day, during a fairly long life, by some act I made others happier, and so spiritualized and uplifted my spirit. Such was my only religion.

"When the separation approached, though I had no actual knowledge of what was to come, I had no fear. I had been very sick, felt greatly exhausted, and longed for rest. I realized the presence of my family and their grief. There came to my senses harmonious vibrations that sounded afar off, like string and reed instruments played by master hands. It seemed to approach and then recede, and was lost. It soothed and comforted me. Then I realized that others were in the room. I could not see their faces distinctly, and wondered at strangers coming in at such a time. Someone spoke, and, rousing up, I saw more clearly and recognized many of my friends whom I had thought dead.

"I was not startled or frightened – it was all so natural. They greeted me cordially and asked me to go with them. Without effort, other than desire, I arose and joined them and went with them, for the moment forgetting the grief of my family. I seemed to travel without effort. Then I met a great company of men and women with radiant faces, clothed in white and blending colors. Their greeting was one of joyous welcome, and happiness was in everything. It was like meeting old friends that had been gone for a long time; it was simply glorious and so intense that for a time I gave no thought to the tremendous import of it all. Then I looked about. There was harmony in everything. I was in a new country. About me I saw great variety of landscape, most picturesque mountain ranges, valleys, rivers, lakes, forests, and the corresponding vegetable life of all that I had known.

It was suggested that I go to a rest house, where my strength would be restored. I did and seemed to fall into a deep sleep almost immediately. After a time I awoke, when some one whom I knew and loved said, "Come with me now and view your inheritance." I went, and the glory of it was, and is, beyond my power of description.

"I should like the privilege some time to tell the world of the beauty in which I live, and the pleasure I find in the work allotted to me. This plane, and all planes, I am told, is governed by law – nature's law, the same as yours – and it is the privilege and duty of every one to develop the spirit by study and helping others. There is much that I should like to say of my return to my family, but, as I am asked only to describe my spirit passage, I will leave that and tell you more concerning the joy of the spirit at some more opportune time.

"There are those in the next life who have qualified for, and are assigned to, the reception department, whose duty it is to solace and comfort such as are grief-stricken because of the sudden severing of social ties, as it seems to those taken suddenly out of the mortal. This is a description:

"I am here to describe as well as I can the actual scenes over here, as the new born spirits, divested of their physical bodies, come over. They come to us, not one or two or three, but in crowds, by thousands and more, some not awakened to consciousness, some just waking, some fully conscious. Few realize for some time that they have passed the portal you call death, but as realization comes and they understand, their thoughts are of their strongest ties. What a commotion of feeling one hears! The same intense feelings exist when out of the old body as when in the physical, and those feelings are just as discernible to spirit sensation as before, only the mode of expression and reception is changed.

"As I was feeling my soul leaving the physical sheath, I heard mysterious chords of rhythmic melody rising and falling like distant waves of the sea. A voice said in thrilling gentleness: "My child, pass from vision into luminous light, from night to day, from death to life." Then a light beating slowly passed away from about me and to my utter amazement I found myself resting at a place quite free and transcendent with divine light. A deep and gentle sound vibrating through the ethereal firmament filled me with joy and happiness, and nothing was perceptible to me except this vibration of the sound. I felt that I must wait till a divine messenger came to guide me into the regions yet unseen.

The atmosphere of awe and reverence that swept over, me for the moment gradually paled away and, rising as I thought, I walked through the darkness which then encompassed me. As I did this, my other hand was suddenly caught by some one in a warm and eager clasp and I was guided along with an infinitely gentle but commanding touch, which I had no hesitation in obeying. Step by step I walked with a strange sense of happy reliance on my companion and guide. Darkness and distance had no misgivings for me. And as I went onward with my hand yet held in that masterful but tender grasp, my thoughts became, as it were, suddenly cleared into a light of full understanding of the celestial world and its joy. And so I went on and on, caring little how long the journey might be and even eagerly wishing that it might continue, when presently a faint light began to peer through darkness, first blue and grey, then white, and then rose. The light, so sublimely luminous, gradually condensed into matter, and in a moment a celestial being of beauty, richly wrapped up in pure white and silken robes, stood before me. After the thrilling sensation, caused by this sudden manifestation, had given a little way for courage and hope, I beheld the same figure transforming into an almost manly and commanding attitude, with radiant face and brilliant eyes now turned towards me. It asked, in a, gentle but firm tone, whether I would like to remain there in the ethereal world and enjoy the pleasures stored up for me as a requital for my past life on the earth plane. Overwhelmed with awe and respect, I could give no answer. Seeing me thus puzzled, my guide placed his right hand upon my forehead and a gentle massage filled me with strength and fresh energy.

"I became bold and courageous, looked my visitor in the eyes, and knelt before him. He lifted me up gently and said I could for a time remain in those ethereal regions where all was pleasure and happiness. He said that the place I was then in was the destination of those who are recruited from amongst people who spend their lives and energy on earth for the sake of their fellow creatures, people who do great deeds for the uplift of the oppressed and harassed, the abode of people who showed equal compassion to both men and beasts. This was my welcome, such my second birth. This was my greeting when I crossed the frontiers of the Afterlife."

4

After Dissolution

WHEN THE END COMES at the close of life's short day, we with loving hands dress the vacant tenement and tenderly and reverently consign it to the earth, from whence it came, again to mingle with the elements. But what of the invisible inner body, the living, thinking individual that has left the physical housing? What is its vision, sensation, thought, experience?

This is best described by one who passed through that change; one who had lived a good life and had necessarily entered into a fine environment. This description was not given me direct, but I can vouch for its truthfulness, for I have verified it. This spirit, describing where she went and what she saw immediately following dissolution, said:

"You wish to know where I went on leaving the earth. Well, there seemed to be a period of unconsciousness; then I awoke and found myself in an entirely different place from any I had known on earth. I was somewhat confused at first; most people are, and find it difficult to realize where they are and what has happened to them. I was not afraid, however, because I had believed I would be taken care of, and would go on living somewhere. My ideas about the afterlife, however, were very vague, as are those of the majority of people. Psychic work will change all that, however, and people will know better what to expect; instead of fearing and dreading the dissolution of the body, as so many millions do now, it will appear to them as it really is, just a sleep and an awakening!

"You are wondering, and have often wondered, why I was taken when I seemed to be, and was, so much needed on earth. You have blamed God, and thought it cruel and hard and not by any means an act of love. This is the result of your limited vision.

"I will give you a description of the place in which I found myself when I awoke after what you call "death." It took me some time to realize the beauty of my surroundings, as my eyes were blinded by the sorrow which my going had caused on earth. The grief of my people kept me so sad at first that I was not able to see or think of anything but earthly sorrow. That is why grief for departed friends and relatives is so wrong, and is so harmful, both to those on earth and to those who come over.

The longer that grief continues and the more hopeless it is, the more those mourned for are kept to earth. Instead of being able to go straight on when they come over, seeing and realizing the beauty and wonders of their surroundings, and helping others to see them also, they are kept in a state of helpless grief, which renders them incapable of helping either themselves or others. Fortunately, the grief of my people on earth was not of this desperately hopeless variety, and I was enabled in time to rise above it and get on with my work of helping others.

"This is a life of service. Self must be eliminated. That is why folk who have lived unselfish lives on earth get on so well here. They do not need the preliminary training which more selfish spirits need. It is a very long time before some spirits who come over are of any use at all in helping others. This is caused partly by their own selfishness and partly by the selfish grief of their friends and relatives on earth. That is why so many of the messages sent through are a plea to those relatives for a more hopeful outlook." All that I have said is necessary that you may better understand what I am about to tell you. When I had been enabled to throw off somewhat the effects of the grief which others felt for my passing, I began to see how beautiful the place I had been brought to was. It is where most spirits go on leaving the earth. They are taken there by other spirits and every effort is made to help them to forget the earth and its cares and worries. This lovely place is called the "Palace of Light," because that is what is most needed by the spirits of human beings when they come over – more light, to enable them to see and understand many things which have not been clear to them while on earth. Human vision – the earthly kind – is very narrow in most cases. People fail to grasp the wonder and beauty even of the earth, so it is no wonder that they need more light and a considerable amount of training before they can see and realize all the beauty and grandeur to be found over here.

"Everything is so surprisingly beautiful that, once their eyes are opened and the full majesty and splendor of it all begins to dawn on them, they are transformed and become beautiful likewise. Once this transformation is accomplished, their training is at an end and they can go on their way rejoicing in all the beauty of their surroundings, helping others to see and realize it too.

"It is almost impossible for us to help some spirits, as they have no desire to be different or better than they have always been. Prayer by those still on the earth is the only thing which can help them. It will give them a desire for better things. Until there is that desire in their hearts, they will remain much as they were when they were in the flesh. Their spirits still inhabit the earth and they are the evil, or sometimes just the mischievous, spirits I have told you about before. Prayer is not only a protection against them, but is also their only hope of salvation. Indifference is the greatest sin there is. As long as folk desire to be better, there is some foundation to build on, but if that desire is lacking it is very difficult to do anything with them.

"I really cannot give you an adequate description of the beautiful Palace of Light. It is so marvelous and so stupendous that it would not be possible for any one still on the earth to grasp its significance. It is not just a building, as the word "Palace" might suggest to your mind. It is a wondrous land of light, where the beauties of nature, as seen on the earth, are brought to perfection. There we have sea, sky, hills, mountains, valleys and grassy plains, in all their beauty of form and coloring, but without blemish. There are no barren or desolate places and there is none of man's handiwork to mar all this loveliness.

"There are forests of noble trees, great rivers, waterfalls, lakes, streams of all sizes, all crystal clear, and lovely meadows carpeted with the most beautiful flowers, over which hover myriads of gorgeous butterflies. There are countless numbers of the most beautiful birds everywhere. Animals of all kinds abound too. Some of them are dainty and graceful, and others are very stately and dignified. It is one vast panorama of loveliness, for those who have eyes to see.

"The great pity is that it is so long before some spirits even begin to see it as it really is. Some of these spirits, who have not progressed far enough to see and realize the beauty about them, when communicating with their friends on earth, give them quite wrong and dissimilar impressions of conditions over here.

"You were wondering just what we mean by the term 'progression'. It is a spiritual condition entirely, and has nothing to do with the place the spirits happen to be in. It is the developing and unfolding of the spiritual nature which is necessary before the spirits concerned can fully appreciate and enjoy the wonderful home prepared for them. Spirits are not obliged to stay in some particular place until they have completed their development. They are all free to go about and see these wonders of which I have been telling you, except that they are not allowed to go and worry the children in their care-free land. Until they develop spiritually, they cannot appreciate all the wonders about them.

"I have not told you anything about the music we get here, except that which the birds make, have I? There is always plenty of beautiful music to listen to. All kinds of instruments are played, and those who desire to do so can play in this great orchestra. Then there is the singing. It is wonderful. Everyone is free to join in this great paean of praise. Those who have not been able to sing as they liked on earth, and have always desired to do better, are able to realize their longing here. It is good to witness their joy over this, when they have progressed sufficiently to hear the singing, and when they are able to join in it their happiness is complete.

"Let it not be inferred that all who have experienced this change have such a delightful experience.

The plane one reaches and the character of one's surroundings depend on the refinement or spirituality of the individual. Each will find the conditions he has fitted himself for, and they are such that money cannot buy. Another has this to say:

"I appreciate your kindness in receiving me so kindly. I speak to you tonight about my experiences in the 'spirit world,' as you call it – I call it the 'higher existence.'

"In describing my passing to the higher, progressive life, I am pleased to say to you that I am giving my own observation, and I do not expect you to accept it as being the testimony of other friends who may have passed over. With what they met, I have nothing to do; I have only to state what I have experienced.

"I may state, concerning my experiences on the earth, that I lived for a long period of time, a little over ninety years, and I led, shall I say, a fairly good life. I should like to say concerning the latter days that, though old in years, I was not at all feeble in body or mind; but as I advanced I felt my powers were failing, and that soon I should be called to leave the scenes of earth for something greater and grander. And so it happened.

"I remember well, on one summer's day, arising in the morning and feeling weak in my body but without pain. It was a weakness, the result of natural decay of the system. And I remember on this occasion that, as the day advanced, I felt more weary. I laid me down upon a couch and fell into a kind of sleep – not a perfect sleep, because I was partially conscious of persons around about me.

"I awoke somewhere about four o'clock in the

afternoon, looked around, and spoke to one or two near me. One was my attendant, who came and asked if I should like something to drink. I said I should. I lay back and waited, and as I did so I felt a strange but not unpleasant feeling coming over me. I can only describe it as a sensuous drowsiness, which seemed too be gaining upon my faculties. The scenes round about me were fading, almost imperceptibly at first, but passing away from me. I was conscious only of that which was just round about me, and then that also seemed to fade away, and my sleep or weakness was merged into sleep which became profound.

"How long that could have continued I do not know, but after a time I again returned to consciousness – these are the only terms I can use to convey to your minds my experiences. Then I realized that I, the Ego, was there just as really as before. I realized that I, the personality, was there, though some change had taken place. I felt as one feels who had dropped something which had burdened him; as a man who had carried a load for a considerable distance, a load that had not been extremely heavy or painful, but still a burden, and I had left it behind somewhere.

"And then, dawning on my spiritual senses, I was conscious that I was in some other state of existence, wherein I was not subject to physical forces as I had experienced them on the earth plane. For instance, the wind did not blow upon me, the sun did not shine, nor did the cold affect me. This I found and experienced with great joy. In place of it I found what you would call, on your mundane sphere, an even temperature, a calm and placid state. I felt that if peace and contentment could be reached, I had reached it. And then I was conscious that round about me there was an innumerable company of people; they were fellow countrymen.

"As I gained a little more experience, or perhaps, as you would say, as my consciousness deepened, I knew that I was attended by spiritual messengers or attendants. Looking to the one on my right, I said – if not openly, I said it within myself, because the Ego speaks within itself, because it is Mind – 'this being is perfection': Divining my thoughts, the guide said to me, 'No, you are being perfected. There is only perfection in the Infinite. Him thou shalt know; with Him thou shalt come in contact,' This helped me considerably. If my guide, my messenger, who was to conduct me through this higher existence, was so perfect in mind, so perfect in every way, what then would be the Author of his perfection? I was satisfied."

5

Where is the Afterlife?

WHERE IS THIS afterlife? Just where do they live? Where are its boundaries? These are questions that I have some difficulty in understanding, and much more in explaining, and I am frank to admit that I have not had all the information sought on this subject. However, I have some knowledge, gained both from my friends in the spirit world and from my ability to deduce from common facts.

Let it be remembered that those in the afterlife have frequently said that every physical thing of this earth was but a poor imitation of what they have there – that all things exist first in the invisible before they can be reproduced in the visible, and that all that we have is a reproduction in form of some of the things that exist there. Here is what one said on this subject:

"We have often told you, and tell you now, that your earth and all things of your earth have their exact counterparts in the spirit world, just as real, just as tangible, just as substantial, to the inhabitants of this world, as material things and forms are to the inhabitants in mortal form upon your earth.

"If this be true, if we have earth and rocks, so do they; if we have shrubs and trees and growing grains and flowers, so do they; if we have houses, schools, great buildings, so do they; if we have oceans, lakes, rivers, and flowing streams, so do they; if this earth is peopled, why not theirs? I am told they have also many things that we have not, as they cannot be clothed in earth garments nor function on our planet.

The density of that plane differs from ours, as the density of our atmosphere differs from that of the water, in which marine life functions. We move more rapidly and with greater freedom than the life that exists in the deep; so those in the higher etheric plane move more rapidly and with greater freedom than we do – all because the material conditions become higher in vibration as we ascend the scale of motion, and there is more resistance the lower we descend.

Striving for more detailed description, I asked a spirit in our work one evening:

"Where is the spirit world? What of its substance, and where are its boundaries?

"The spirit answered:

"It is difficult to explain to you who know little of matter, the location and boundaries of the various planes where we live. First let me impress upon you the fact that energy, that is, life, cannot express itself except in substance. The idea that spirit people function without substance and that they and the plane in which they live are unsubstantial, is preposterous and illogical. The gases that compose water, taken separately, are as substantial as when united. Why should it be thought impossible, since matter was created, for Nature to create other material than physical, to create spirit material? There are millions of worlds inhabited by human beings in that space you call the sky. Don't for a moment think that yours is the only world, and that God made the universe for you alone.

"This spirit world is in reality just as much a part of your planet as the earth and rocks you tread upon.

Around and about your globe, and forming a part of it, are separate, material, concentric belts or zones, varying in width and vibratory action, and therefore in density, into which all mankind and all planetary life pass, on the happening of that event you call death.

"I only know the boundaries of these planes in which I live and labor. I do not know any more about the boundaries of the planes beyond me than you know of the planes beyond you.

"Others have reported of these localities as follows:

"Your earth has belts, but they exist in a cruder condition than those of Jupiter and Saturn. The belts or zones that lie around your earth are designed for the habitation of spirits out of the body; and as they outgrow the passions of earth and become more refined, they pass to another or higher zone.

"I have discovered, while living here, that there are several magnetic belts encircling your earth, similar in general appearance to the belts that surround the planet Jupiter, and beyond those zones there exists, outside earth's spirit sphere, a vast spirit world traversing the innermost heart of space.

Another said:

"I, too, am permitted to gaze back in this way at earthly scenes; and, for a time, to dwell on earthly memories while bringing to you for your world some experiences and observations of my own, both in mortal existence and in the spheres.

"I have observed that there are innumerable states and conditions and diversified experiences in spirit as on earth. We may illustrate by different highways, thus:

"Let one condition be represented by a certain

highway, and another condition by another and differing highway, leading through a different country.

"As no two highways of your world lead over the same country and present the same scenery to the traveler, so of the children of earth no two travel over the same highway or have the same experiences; to each are presented different scenes from those presented to any other.

"One person traveling one road is landed into the spirit world at one point, and one on another road enters spirit life at another point; and a third, on yet another road, enters at a different point from either of the others. And so on the endless procession moves, landing its infinitude of differentiated individualities; and each one has a different idea to relate. Therefore no two relate the same story of the earthly journey.

"But the varied highways of earth continue into eternity, and the traveler on each goes eternally on his own road from the earth life. And thus all travel on in the spirit world, having different experiences here, as with you; and, on returning to you, we have different experiences and different descriptions of the spirit world to relate to you, according as each has realized for himself"

This is another spirit's report:

"There are seven concentric rings called spheres.

The region nearest the earth is known as the first or rudimental sphere. It really blends with your earth sphere. It is just one step higher in vibration. Growing more intense and increasing in action are six more, distinguished as the spiritual spheres. Theses are all zones or circles of exceeding fine matter encompassing the earth like belts or girdles – each separate from the other and regulated by fixed laws. They are not shapeless fancies or mental projections, but absolute entities, just as tangible as the planets of the solar system, or the earth on which you reside. They have latitude and longitude and atmosphere of peculiarly vitalized vapor. The undulating currents, soft and balmy, are invigorating and pleasurable.

"Although the spheres revolve with the earth on a common axis, forming the same angle with the plane of the ecliptic, and move with it about your sun, they are not dependent upon that sun for either light or heat; they receive not a perceptible ray from that ponderable source.

"We receive our light emanations," he said, "wholly from a great central source, from which comes uninterrupted splendor, baffling description.

"I can readily appreciate that spirit people along the Frontier and among the rudimentary spheres cannot tell how many there are beyond, and may not all agree, but here is what another says on the subject:

"There are innumerable spheres in the spirit world. If it were not so, progression would be a myth. Some tell you that there are only seven. That is because they have no knowledge beyond that sphere. I do not mean a place fixed by boundaries, for the spheres or degrees in spirit life are only conditions and are not confined to a limited space; as a soul develops, it naturally arises above its surroundings and consequently experiences a change in its spheres or conditions.

"Impressed with the suggestion concerning Jupiter and Saturn, I examined the works of the foremost astronomers, and this is, in substance, what they say:

Jupiter is marked with bands, more or less wide,

more or less intense, which show perfectly near its equatorial region. Saturn has a number of what appear to be broad, flat rings surrounding it, but separated from it on all sides, which lie all in the same plane of inclination to the ecliptic. The inner and broader of the two belts or zones is the brightest near the outer part, and shades off toward the planet – gradually at first, more rapidly afterward. Its inner portion is so dark that at one time it was regarded separate and called "Crape" or "dusty" ring. Modern telescopes show the inner part of this ring transparent.

The physical constitution of the rings is unlike that of any other known objects in our solar system. They are not formed of a continuous mass of solid or liquid matter, but of discrete particles of unknown minuteness, probably widely separated in proportion to their individual volume, yet so close as to appear continuous.

To know the location of the next plane helps one to appreciate conditions that exist there. Our finite minds can comprehend little that we have not actually experienced, and so we mentally grope in our efforts to comprehend what is told us of those more advanced spheres, and must in a measure rely on deductive reasoning. I also have found that spirit people do not agree in many respects, any more than we do. Each reports according to his knowledge and understanding; therefore, each must form his own conclusions, based on reason.

In order to get another expression, I read what I have written to Dr. David Hossack, one of the leaders of the spirit group with whom I worked so many years, and for whose statements I have great respect, and in reply he said:

What appears as space about your earth is composed of ether. There are three distinct circles, the outer filled with more radiant vibrations than those within. Beyond these, the spheres or circles blend with those of other planets. Each circle is very, very many miles in depth, according to your standard of measurement.

"I am much impressed with such statements, as they seem natural and appeal to reason. So far as I know, no one has heretofore attempted actually to locate and fix the boundaries of the afterlife.

Two thousand years of Christian teaching have not enabled a reasoning mind to form any definite conclusions as to where that place called heaven is, or concerning the conditions prevailing where the so-called dead reside, and it seems quite time that we have a scientific explanation, or at least a start along the road.

When Columbus discovered the continent of North America, the whole world at once accepted the fact, changed their ideas about the earth's shape, and still celebrate his achievement. The psychic investigators within the last seventy-five years have discovered not a continent but millions of inhabited worlds, and now actually locate the planes, begin to understand the substances that compose them, and know something of the light that fills those zones, achievements that transcend all discoveries of modern times. Our descriptions, so concise and brief, but serve as texts, however, and from them we must make deductions and bring understanding to ourselves.

It will be noted that there is a similarity between the circles or rings about our earth, and those of Jupiter and Saturn. Our astronomers contend that these circles or rings are not formed of a continuous mass of solid or liquid substance, but of discrete particles of unknown minuteness, unlike any other visible objects in our solar system. These statements demonstrate that matter has phases or conditions not generally understood by earth dwellers.

Those who have spoken – Faraday, Denton and Hossack, and others above quoted – are in a position to know something of the substance that fills that plane, and they all say it is ether. And what is ether? Our encyclopedias explain it as the upper, purer air; the abode of the gods. Our astronomers say that it is a hypothetical medium of extreme tenuity and elasticity, supposed to be diffused throughout all space. Spirit people say that ether is matter similar to earth substance, but in a very high state of vibration. According to them, the universe is all material, substance or matter in different and varying states of vibration, and those rings, circles or envelopes that surround this earth of ours are just as substantial, visible, real and tangible as anything we have. Those zones vibrate in substantially direct proportion to our thoughts, and may well be called the mental plane.

No thoughtful person can read these statements from distinguished and scientific spirits without being impressed, and without drawing from them rational deductions. Beyond the visible is the true field of discovery. Here secrets are veiled from physical sight, and the mental powers, based on the statements of spirit people, are the only means available to push discovery to its ultimate.

I know that these gentlemen made the statements quoted. The world counted them not only honest but great scientists, when they resided here. Their statements appear in accordance with nature's tendency. They are rational and I accept them, and, basing my opinion thereon and on other knowledge obtained from persons in the afterlife, I state without qualification that about this earth there are material concentric belts or zones, composed of ether, which become more radiant and higher in vibration as they extend outward. In these zones all the so-called dead reside and have their homes, where the family relation is ultimately restored. For the first time the local habitations of spirit people have been discovered and the spheres or zones can now be named.

6

Voices of the Dead

I N 1890, ON THE trial of an action before one of
our Judges, he called me to the bench during an
intermission, and exhibited some slates that pur-
ported to contain messages from dead people. I examined them, and laughed at the suggestion. This was immediately followed by a statement that the night before
he had talked, voice to voice, with them. I was incensed
that he should state such an absurd proposition; I felt
that if communication with the dead was possible, it
would have been known from the beginning. Filled
with indignation, I turned and went on with the trial.
This man stood high in the community, had the appearance of being sane, and I could not account, at the
time, for what seemed to me an irrational mental condition. I am wondering whether or not some who read
this presentation will not, at first, view my statements
as I viewed those of this able judge.

It is a fact to be noted, that every man's vision, everyone's conception, is to him normal, and, when a fact
is stated that is not within his experience or in accord
with his understanding, the tendency is to contradict
and ridicule, rather than to investigate, weigh, and consider with an open mind, fairly and without prejudice.

I did not then know that a seed had been planted in
fertile soil, and, though I then condemned it and later,
with all my mental powers alert, endeavored to destroy
it, that the time would come when from actual experience I should comprehend the truth of such contention

and should understand how it was done. My early experience prevents me from criticizing others who do not and cannot now accept as true what is here stated as a fact.

Comprehension and acceptance of these discoveries, so beyond the average experience, must be of slow growth, and come from individual research and deductive reasoning; but it may now be said that there is much more known, and more literature on this subject, than when I commenced my research work. Therefore knowledge can be more quickly obtained.

In my early efforts to disprove what was, to my mind, a growing evil, I examined every known method by which it was claimed that those in the afterlife could communicate with those in this life. I will treat the more important methods in what follows.

Table Tipping
Whenever spirit people get a message through, they must utilize what Crookes terms "psychic force." All persons do not possess it, but ordinarily about one in five does. If that number sit about a table, with hands upon it, frequently spirits can intelligently answer questions by tapping or by actual movement of the table. This is the most primitive and, at the same time, the most undesirable of all methods, because of the difficulty of obtaining proof of identity. Spirit people deliberately, and sometimes mischievously, impersonate a person asked for, and, when this is discovered, doubt is cast on the genuineness of the manifestation. Scientific investigators do not advise such practice.

Planchette and Ouija Board

These can be operated only by one who likewise possesses psychic or mediumistic abilities. Spirit people, using that force in conjunction with their own, operate these instruments, but they are open to the same objections as the process above mentioned and should be operated only by those who understand the process fully. In their use, much that is unreliable is obtained. This does not condemn the phenomena, but lessens the value of the results obtained.

Slate Writing

There is no question about the genuineness of this phenomenon, but few possess that peculiar force which is needed for this purpose. When a psychic is found like Pierre Keeler, now of Washington, spirits can write between slates by his aid with great freedom. One of my first experiments was with this man, at which time I received a message in handwriting that I recognized. I could not then accept what I received as in fact a message from the beyond. It was beyond my experience then, but I know now that this method, with an honest medium, is reliable.

Clairvoyance Clairaudience

The first is the ability of one still in the physical body to see, and the latter is the ability psychically to hear, spirit people, and to tell how they look, who they are, and to repeat what they say. Usually a psychic or medium possesses both faculties. With an honest medium, spiritually and properly developed, this method is reliable, otherwise it is not.

Trance

There are two phases of this condition. The complete trance occurs when a spirit causes the body of the medium temporarily to vacate the physical tenement, of which for the moment it takes possession, using the medium's physical organs of speech. Then there is the semi-trance, where the medium tells what he sees, and what spirit people say. Communication, in this manner, is possible, but it is not always satisfactory because of the opportunity for deceit. It is under this guise that fortune-tellers prey on the public, to the detriment of this philosophy and to the loss of the dupes who patronize them. I am told by my spirit friends that spirit people know no more of events which will occur in the future than we do; therefore, the laws that prohibit fortune-telling by ignorant and dishonest persons are just and necessary. That unfortunate practice has brought this whole work into disrepute in the minds of many people, and every earnest investigator deeply regrets it.

Automatic Writing

In the hands of a fine man or woman, spiritually developed and honest, this method is very useful. Phases of mediumship differ, so that we seldom find a psychic that has more than one phase. It seems to require different psychic force for the different methods. There are two phases of this method: the first, where a person goes into a complete trance, in which case spirit people manipulate the hand and actually write; the second, where the psychic is fully conscious; in this case the messages and answers to questions are suggested to, and heard through, his subconscious brain, dictated, as I dictate to my stenographer.

Materialization

Physical demonstrations are possible. Spirit people under certain conditions can, and do, temporarily clothe their bodies with a physical substance, so that they are, for the moment, visible, and, to the touch, natural. This also requires the presence of a medium from whom a force or substance is taken, as it is taken from others present.

The Direct or Independent Voice

This is by far the most satisfactory method of all, for the voice is recognized, and it is easy to prove identity in this manner. This requires darkness, but so sensitive is the condition required the vibrations must be slower than in daylight, and, they are in a darkened room.. In this method, the organs of speech of a spirit are temporarily clothed with physical substance taken in part from those present and from the psychic. The spirit group contribute also, and the combined substance blended together is precipitated on the vocal organs of the spirit person. Then the voice of a spirit actually reaches our ears. But for this condition, though spirits might speak they would not be heard by one who, like myself, does not possess mediumistic powers.

There are many mediums who have something of this ability. There are, however, only a few so highly developed that the voices are heard clear, strong and full, as in earth life. I worked many years improving the mediumship of Mrs. French, so that the voices of spirit people came full-toned. We succeeded in accomplishing this, and for many years, until the dissolution of this wonderful psychic, I talked not with a hundred but with thousands of spirits, a majority of whom, perhaps, I had intimately known in their earth life. It would require many volumes to print the record obtained in all the years of my research work. I am not attempting to do so; I simply state as a fact that I have done these things, and explain how it is done, in hope that the facts will appeal to reason, through which all knowledge comes. I hope that what I write will be of such character and dignity, and will so appeal to the common sense of the public, that they will think rather than condemn.

So mighty is the force of human thought, and so delicate are the conditions of a spirit's body when it has taken on material in preparation for speech, that, by word of command, or even by thought projection, I can break down conditions and prevent speech. This is why those who oppose this philosophy so often get negative results when they seek demonstration, for by their mental attitude or thought-conditions they make impossible the very thing they seek; they so intensify their thought substance that spirit-people are not able to break into the conditions they make for the occasion.

Each voice has individuality. When new spirits come for the first time and take on the condition of vocalization, there is often a similarity in tone quality, but this soon passes away, as they grow accustomed to using their voices in this way. The voices of those accustomed to speak never change, and are easily recognized. There is no similarity of thought or words. These differ with different people in that world as in this.

The strength of the voices varies greatly. One of our group always speaks with sufficient volume to fill easily a great auditorium, and his lectures ring through the whole house. Another, whom I have in mind, always comes with great courtesy, is careful in speech and considerate; but his voice, while very distinct, has no great volume. The voice of another, who was very near to me in earth life, is as clear, strong and natural as in the days when we discussed this philosophy, or walked in the forest about the cabin, trying to come in touch with the principle of life; and since his going we have talked as much, and with as great freedom, as in the latter years before his going. There has been no subject of knowledge common to us both, that he ever hesitated to discuss in all its minutest details. This friendship of many years is continued without a break, and I have enjoyed his presence and our talks as I never did before.

One evening a stranger spoke, who said he was a physician of Philadelphia., He was brought in that help might be given to complete the separation from his physical body. When he finally became fully conscious, he told his name, the number of his residence, and much about himself. The papers the next morning had a full account of his death early the evening before.

In the beginning, much time was wasted in proving the identity of strange spirits who were allowed to talk, and in verifying what they said concerning themselves. I know that spirit-people, as a rule, are as prone to deceive as mortals. At one time, few men of my acquaintance passed on who did not come and speak with me; but later the time was devoted to obtaining more information concerning this new philosophy, that the greatest good might come to the greatest number.

Hundreds, at my invitation, have participated in the work and with me have heard different voices with different tones, different thoughts, different personalities, and at times in different foreign languages.

No spirit was at liberty to come into our room without the invitation of the spirit-group or of myself, any more than a stranger would come into my house uninvited for social purposes. The same laws of privilege and hospitality which operate in the earth life prevail in the spirit world.

There was opposition to this work in spirit spheres in the beginning, just as it is opposed now in this world. Some churches exist as institutions in the afterlife, and are just as jealous of their domination there as here. In our earliest work these opponents often tried to prevent speech by interrupting and disorganizing the circle, fearing that the truth might cause loss of temporal as well as spiritual power both here and there. Great efforts were made by the spirit-group and ourselves to maintain conditions and keep them out. I recall one evening, when my stenographer was taking a lecture in shorthand, that a Catholic priest in the spirit world gained admittance. Such was his strength that he suddenly wrenched the stenographic book from the hands of the stenographer, and threw it with great violence against the wall of the room. Our group finally forced him out and, as he was leaving, I heard him say," What can one man do among so many millions?"

What a privilege was mine. Night after night, through long years, with the aid of Emily S. French, I talked with thousands of the living dead, in my own home, and from them I learned all that I am telling here – learned more than I can ever write.

Remember that spirit-people have the same inner body as when it was physically housed in this earth-life, and, given the required help, can, and will, speak as before. If this may be said to be a new discovery, it is of greater importance than any since the dawn of civilization.

7

Materiality of the Universe

I T IS MOST DIFFICULT for the human mind to comprehend that anything which sight or sense does not disclose is material. The idea that what we call space is substantial and real, and composed of matter, the same as those things that are visible, presents a proposition difficult of acceptance – we know so little of matter's physical properties.

If those in the afterlife live and progress in a world as substantial and material as this, have houses and other structures and buildings, if that plane has forests and fields and growing grain, flowers, mountains, meadow lands and flowing streams, then that world is as substantial and real and composed of the same substance as this, varying only in vibratory action. As a matter of fact, these two worlds or conditions now blend, one with the other. What we see, feel and touch, only clothes visible life. Through nature, as we use that word, the spirit world functions and has temporary physical expression. This fact science is just coming to understand, but as yet little is known of the constituent parts of matter that fill the Universe, whether physical or spiritual.

Heretofore matter has been known in but three conditions – solid, liquid and gaseous. Sir William Crookes, the learned English chemist, while endeavoring to create a vacuum in a glass tube, discovered a fourth condition, which he named the radiant state. The atoms, freed by rarefaction, assume in this relative vacuum vibratory motions of intense and incalculable rapidity. They become flambent and produced effects of light and electrical radiations. This suggests a clue to most of the cosmic phenomena.

Variously condensed, in its three first conditions, matter in the radiant state loses a number of its properties, such as density, shape, color and weight; but in this new found realm, it appears to be more closely and intimately related to the force which is life. This fourth aspect is another condition which matter is susceptible of assuming. The mind can picture a subtle, hyper fluidic state, as superior to the radiant condition as the radiant is superior to the gaseous, or the liquid to the solid. Science will in the future solve this problem and find an answer to such age-long and formidable problems as the unity of substance, or the preponderating forces of the universe.

Matter, in its higher and more refined vibrations, becomes a fluid of infinite suppleness and elasticity, by endless combinations of which all bodies are engendered. In its primordial essence – invisible, impalpable, imponderable – this fluid, through successive transitions, becomes ponderable and capable of producing, by powerful condensation, those hard, opaque and weighty bodies which constitute the base of terrestrial matter. This state of cohesion is, however transitory. Matter, reascending the ladder of its transformations, can as readily be disaggregated and returned to its primitive fluidic state.

All matter is composed of molecules, atoms and electrons. The smallest particle that can be detected by the human eye through the microscope is about twenty-five times larger than a molecule.

The molecule is composed of atoms which individually are about one three-hundred-millionth of an inch in diameter, while the electron – as the ultimate subdivision of matter – has a diameter 100,000 less than the atom. There would be thirty trillions of electrons to the inch, each one clothing life, that is force.

It must, therefore, be admitted first of all that nothing we see around us is absolutely solid. A mass of anything, whether it is metal, rock or other apparently dense and solid substance, does not exist as such. Cohesion of particles is relative only in proportion to weight, and each particle of a mass is relatively distant from the others, allowing space for the free passage of the ether, light – such as the X-ray-radio energy, which is life expressed in substance.

Professors Thompson and Tait say that if a drop of water could be magnified to the size of the earth, we should see the atoms about as big as oranges, and that electrons are about a thousand times smaller. Sir William Crookes, when elected President of the British Association for the Advancement of Science, in 1898, said in a remarkable address that all of the phenomena of the universe are presumably continuous waves, and that we have good evidence that they range from one vibration to two thousand trillions per second, thus varying in their frequency and also in their velocity. As a starting point he said,

"I will take a pendulum beating seconds in air. If I keep on doubling, I get a series of steps, as follows:

Starting point

Step	Vibrations per second	
1	2	
2	4	
3	8	
4	16	
5	32	
6	64	
7	128	
8	256	Sound
9	512	
10	1,024	
15	32,768	
20	1,048,576	
25	83,554,432	Electrical-rays
30	1,073,741, 824	
35	34,359,738,368	
40	1,099,511,627,776	Unknown
45	85,184,872,088,832	
50	1,125,899,906,842,624	Heat-light rays
55.	36,028,707,018,963,968	Unknown
58	288,230,376,151,711,744	
59	576,440,752,203,423,488	Roentgen, or X-rays
61	2,305,763,009,213,693,952	
62	4,611,526,018,427,385,904	Radium rays
63	9,223,052,036,854,775,808	

"It will be seen by the above that at the fifth step from unity, at thirty-two vibrations per second, we reach the region where atmospheric vibration reveals itself to us in sound. At 32,768 per second, to the average human ear, the region of sound ends.

After the 32nd step vibration increases rapidly,

giving us electric waves, then light waves at an unthinkable number of vibrations per second, until we reach the X-ray and finally, to us, the radium ray. The rays of radium are the results of quintillions of vibrations per second, and are also so subtle that they pass through all solids. It may be that the X-waves and the radium waves are only at the threshold of the wonders of the unseen universe. It seems to me in these rays we may have a possible mode of transmitting intelligence, which, with a few reasonable postulates, may supply a key to much that is obscure in psychical research.

"Force, or energy, is life and is composed of and functions in matter on both planes. It is only when energy, or life, takes on a covering of gross material that it functions physically. Like all else in nature, it is indestructible; energy or life is found in and functions in every stratum. It does not begin at the earth's surface nor end in the air. Life differs in every condition of matter – in the earth, on the earth, and in that vast expanse which we ignorantly call space. The difficulty is that we do not as yet understand the various conditions and constituent parts of the matter in which the universe is expressed and functions. Until we do, we cannot understand how the so-called dead live and labor in a world material, tangible and real.

The subject is perhaps the most complicated of any in nature. Its mystery is at present beyond any man's comprehension. I but hope to create an interest in the subject, to set in motion individual thought. Others may, by research, work out some conception of the conditions in which those who have gone before live and work from day to day. We are coming to the conclusion that force and thought blend one with the other, that all are expressed in substance and are an expression of life force.

Water is a transparent, inodorous and tasteless fluid. It is a compound substance, consisting of hydrogen and oxygen in the proportion of two to one – by weight, two parts of hydrogen to sixteen parts of oxygen. These are both gases. Atmosphere is likewise a gas, is inodorous, invisible, insipid, colorless, elastic and, being substance, is possessed of gravity. It is composed by volume of twenty-one parts of oxygen and seventy nine of nitrogen, mixed but not chemically united.

From the generic rock we see matter ascending in its vibratory condition, step by step, to the earth's surface; then the water with faster movement than air; then the ether, no less substance than are atmosphere and water, about which as yet we know but little. The component parts of ether are not known to certainty, but that it is substance is admitted. Ether, as we now know, fills all space and is the medium of light, heat and sound. It not only fills space, but passes through all solids; so intense are its vibrations. It is not strange that we do not see it, for we cannot see atmosphere. The reason we see water is because of its slow vibration. We do not see electricity, except as we reduce the speed of its vibration. Therefore, it is not strange that we are unable to see ether.

Each stratum has its form of life. The earth has worms and crawling things, the sea fish and other marine life, the air man and animal life, the ether spirit people – each condition, each environment, is natural and real, and all are according to the divine plan. Today our physical bodies have a density, substantially corresponding to other substances, which limits our movements. Tomorrow, when the inner or etheric body emerges from its present housing, it will vibrate in accord with the finer etheric conditions, which are now invisible to us. All this is as natural to spirit people as things of the world are to us.

What I am trying to explain is that the universe is substance, or matter, real and substantial. We are now clothed with physical substance; we function and work on one plane, the earth plane. The spirit people live and labor on another, a higher plane. They are separated from us, just as we are separated from various forms of life below us. This afterlife – Heaven, if you use that term – is substantial, composed of matter higher in vibration than the air in which we function. And in that vitalized, material condition, spirit people live just as we do, build structures of the varying substances, and grow things exactly as we do, though with greater freedom.

In calling attention to the constituent and chemical properties of our material, I show how little we know of matter, and lead, step by step, through its increasing intensity and vibration, in order that we may in a small measure comprehend the material conditions in which spirit people live.

We do not comprehend that substance called ether, and probably will not understand it until we become inhabitants of that plane, but we do know it is a substance and reality, as people live and labor in surroundings as real and tangible to them as the earth's substance is to us.

Another, speaking of the materiality of the next plane, has said:

"Spirit ether fills the universe. It is a compound of

two coexistent, coeternal elements, the one positive, the other negative; one the male, the other the female element. These two primitive elements do exist, and always have existed, in union. Organic life is an aggregation of these primitive, spiritual elements. The law of chemical affinity, of every form of cohesion, of every human desire, of all love and affection, is but a manifestation of the amity of positive and negative spirit ether asserting itself in organic aggregations of the positive and negative spirit atoms. Suns and systems of worlds are organic evolutions of this eternal life element. Spirit ether fills the universe. Life permeates and is inherent in all things. Nature expresses all there is of creative energy."

Another inhabitant of the next plane, speaking of matter spiritual and physical, says:

"Our world is composed of matter as real and definite as your own, but that matter vibrates at a higher rate, consequently your undeveloped senses can have but little cognizance of it. And, your own sphere being composed of matter at a low rate of vibration, it is almost equally as difficult for us to manifest on your plane as it is for you to penetrate ours. Yet we have evolved from your plane, and have all the experience of that evolution, and it is perhaps easier for us to reach back and help you than it is for you to see forward. The principle of co-operation between the two planes is what we desire to establish, for this principle of co-operation is an essential and necessary condition for the development of the consciousness from your low and stagnant vibrations to those that are higher and healthier and more in keeping with the spirit's deepest longing, more in harmony with that process that is working for the ultimate and absolute destiny of the evolving spirit of man.

"How little we know, and how much there is yet to learn of that which we call matter or substance in nature; until the mentality grasps in some measure this subject, life beyond can not be comprehended."

8

Light in the Spirit World

THERE WERE FEW nights in all the years of my research that Dr. David Hossack did not address us on some subject. He always came with charming courtesy and great cordiality. His voice was low, but he spoke clearly and to the point. No more distinguished or delightful guest ever entered my home. It will be noted that I make no distinction in speaking of those who enter my home. It matters not whether for the moment they function in the spirit or in the physical plane; they are all people and can discuss questions, when proper conditions are provided, with equal freedom. During the period when I obtained these discourses from the beyond, I formed or provided the conditions requisite and necessary, as I have explained elsewhere.

The question of light in the next world has always interested me, and it is one of the subjects upon which I have sought information. I speak of Dr. Hossack, for the reason that he has given me the most satisfactory explanation of any. This was my question to him:" What is the character of your light, and how does it differ from sunlight?"

The answer:

"The light we have is obtained from the action of our minds on the atmosphere. We think light, and there is light. That is why people who come over in evil condition are in the dark; their minds are not competent to produce light enough for them to see.

"There is greater intensity of light as we go up through the spheres, which comes from the blending of the more spiritual minds.

"Our life is merely the condition of mind which each one has. We create images in thought, and have the reality before us, just as tangible as your houses and buildings are to you. You do not have any conception of the great power and force there is, or may be, in thought. It dominates all conditions and makes us what we are. One who realizes this may control his destiny.

"Thought is a fluid, which becomes substance to us when once it is formed into an expression. It is a vibrating, living thing, and should be recognized as such and controlled accordingly.

Another spirit speaks of light as follows:

"When you speak of the sun in the spirit world, you mistake, for there is no such thing. There is light here, radiated from the atoms. Our light is very different from your sun. Your light is grosser than ours; it is unnatural to us, and, therefore, painful to the spirit. Our light is soft, radiant and very brilliant. Your physical eye can never behold it; it is so ethereal, so beautiful, that it blends with sensation.

"But why? What natural law produces spirit light? If this were explained in detail, nothing would be left for deductive reasoning. These descriptions but serve to spur one on to greater effort, and must, of necessity, make deductions and partly by that process understand spirit conditions. I have ever noticed that in seeking knowledge of afterlife conditions, something is left for one to do if he would attain the desired result. This is in accordance with the oft-repeated statement that the spirits only help others to help themselves.

Another's understanding follows:

"There is a great central force, the rays from which gradually lessen in their vibratory action. This force comes from the outside of your world, as you call it, and reaches the lowest ebb in the center of your earth. This central vibratory action is in the highest sphere, and is so intense and vivid that the souls who are in the finest state of development are the only ones who come near its circle. It is the apex of the universe, and that is why there are lesser degrees as it is rayed out through infinite space. These vibrations of light reach the earth and all the other spheres, and the vibratory action of light on each planet depends on its distance from the seat of this creative or central force.

"Some of the planets are much higher in vibratory action than is your earth, and if you were to go to them, and could still retain the earth conditions surrounding you, as usual you could not see any life because your vibration would be so much lower. The need of this condition is so apparent when once one grasps the immensity of the universe and the harmony of its laws.

"If you were able to see all the conditions and people beyond you, life would be chaos and confusion each sphere mixing with another – with no regulations nor harmony anywhere. As it is, each has its own place in the scheme of progression, and this visible wall of vibratory force is the safety guard to continued rational living.

"This force is life, intense, vibrating, dominant. In conception there is the merest touch to this elemental force; consequently, life is forwarded and the continuation of the species insured. It is something discernible as a part of nature and nature is but an expression of this great force.

"Those souls that progress through each step are slowly, but surely, becoming a part of that great force which is life; life itself is light, and ultimately individuality will be lost in the immensity of that great, harmonious life force and will become, in turn, a tiny part of the new conception in the earth form again. I do not mean that this is reincarnation. An atom only is needed to create life in the lower earth forms, and that is taken from the immense whole. This is the law of the universe. There seem no words to tell you, or to make you understand clearly, the plan and purpose of creation; one must accept it and try to realize that one's own life, seemingly so important to one's self, is in reality such a little thing in the immensity of the universe, and yet just as essential to the whole as one petal of a flower is to the perfect rose. It is a part of the perfect whole, and necessary.

"Make that part that is developed by you clean and wholesome, and the going on will be filled with beauty; it will be but the going into a new country, among good friends and great advantages, along spiritual and harmonious lines. But to those who live in the dark and do evil and selfish things, the going will be along rough and stormy places and the helping hand hard to find'

We know so little of light. We have always had the sun, but even now know little about it. Man first devised the torch, which not so long ago was all he had; then came the candle; then whale oil and the lamp; next petroleum assisted man; and, within our own time, he has invented the electric light – evolution of the primitive torch. The ether itself is light, as is evidenced by the fact that the dynamo draws from the atmosphere this substance and condenses it. We may behold electricity, which is a physical expression of the ether that fills all space in the whole universe. The more a man knows, the more he is willing to learn. The less a man knows, the more positive he is that he knows everything.

The question of light is a legitimate field of inquiry, in which any man may make researches, as little has been told concerning it. The suggestion that there is light of another character and that life itself is the light which lights the spirit world, is no more startling than that made concerning the electric lamp a few years ago. There are still many things in nature that we do not know, with all our boasted knowledge.

Our sun is physical. All that is visible is physical, but nothing physical enters the planes that surround this globe. As I understand, nothing physical is visible to spirit people unless they descend into the earth or to lower spirit planes; then they visualize as when in the body. There are countless numbers of spirits also that for ages never rise above earth conditions nor see the radiance of the higher spheres.

A great law governs spirit, as well as physical, sight. A beautiful, tender, loving thought radiates and goes out from the mentality in long, undulating waves. The longer the thought wave, the finer the thought, the higher its vibrations and the lighter in substance, but a selfish thought sends out a short wave, and, because of its deficient length, it is dark. The mind is a shuttle and is ever weaving about us a condition that will surround us completely on the day of our dissolution. If we develop our minds along fine lines, the thought that goes forth from the soul in the next life will illuminate the path of our progression, but if we fail to observe that law, we pay the penalty, for each soul furnishes all the light discernible along its own pathway in the spheres beyond.

The source of life – that is, the source of energy – does not seem to be known by spirits. Only the infinite can comprehend the infinite. They simply know, as I gather, that there is a great, central source of power from which emanates the life force that finds expression in the various places of consciousness. They know something of conditions that exist in the plane on which, for the time, they live, and, just as we of the earth, they labor for a better understanding of nature's wonderful laws. Our progression to this next sphere will not change our ambitions or desires, or our comprehension; and vision – what we see will depend on the light that our souls will radiate. We cannot touch a button or turn a switch and light our way, nor can we borrow a lamp. Self-effort and a clean life along right lines will light the way where the great law places us when the night comes after earth's fitful struggles are over.

9

Homes in the Afterlife

O NE IN THE AFTERLIFE gave me a description of the spirit home of a great, splendid mother, built by the labor of love and ceaseless charity, in the physical as well as in the spirit plane in which she now resides. She worked long and earnestly to make women understand the truth, so that they might live nearer to the best in nature. Here is the description as it was given to me:

"Before me is the interior of a splendid home, the home made by a spirit, created and built by the thoughts, acts and works of one who, thirty-two years ago, lived on the material plane. The room opening before me seems like pure white marble with lofty ceilings. Around the four sides runs a broad balcony supported by columns gracefully turned. From a point beyond the centre is a broad stairway curving outward; at its foot, on each side, are niches filled with beautiful statuary. Going up the stairs now, I find each step a different color, yet all blending as one. On all sides of this upper gallery are windows, through which come soft rays of light. Opening off the sides are rooms; and, as I look, a door opens and a beautiful spirit comes out. She takes on, as she enters, the old, material condition that she may be recognized. She has reached maturity, and has a face of rare gentleness, the beauty of purity. She smiles as we describe her and her home to you. With her is a daughter just reaching womanhood; one that never lived the earth life, who was prematurely born.

These two, drawn by the invisible bond of affection, have built this home and made it rich with love.

"Passing down the corridor now, the mother's arm about the daughter, they approach the other end of the building and descend a stairway similar to the first, and go out upon a broad terrace, along walks bordered with flowers, into the garden of happiness. Turning now and looking toward a valley, I see many trees heavy with foliage, and through them I behold the waters of a lake, rich as an emerald in color.

"About the vaulted room which I have described are many others of like material, filled with all that this mother loves. Books that she uses in her work are seen; pictures, created by acts of tenderness, adorn the wall. Musical instruments, unlike those of earth, await her spirit touch. This is a home where girls just budding into womanhood are taught purity; it is a mother's home, and suggests to you the possibilities of spiritual surroundings. It was not built in a day, but is the result of labor in the earth and in spheres of progression, where the surroundings are in harmony with spiritual development, the home of a good woman, built by helping others.

"I said to one of my friends in the afterlife, at another time:

"Tell me of homes of spirit people." In reply, he said:

"That is a most difficult thing to do, because earth people expect to find everything so different, while, in reality, the homes here are practically the same as in earth life, except that there is in the advanced spheres no discord, no lack of harmony, nothing but light, beauty, music, laughter, blended with earnest, thoughtful study. I am describing the home of a spirit who has grown to know and live within the life-principle. There are many poor, struggling souls, willfully or ignorantly looking down instead of upward, who are living in squalid huts which their deeds and thoughts in earth life have made for them. Very few have beautiful homes ready for them when they enter spirit life, for most people live in such ignorance of natural laws that they find insufficient shelter awaiting them; but, the wise ones start to build by perfecting their way of thinking and by undoing wrongs on earth, and also by helping others. No actual physical touch is given these homes, but, as the soul grows in beauty of thought and deed, the home grows to perfection.

"I asked:

"Are these homes as real to you as ours are to us?"

And he replied:

"They are the abiding places of spirits who gather into them the objects of beauty which they love, and there, harmonious spirits come and go, as in earth life. They are as real to them as yours are to you. But we look at things differently; we think them, and the thought is expressed in waves that are visible and real as long as we hold the thought.

"This is no flight of imagination. Let me bring home the truth by an illustration. Yesterday I purchased a country-place, which must be modernized and adapted to our requirements. I have been thinking what changes are possible and what I should like. It was a mental effort to take into consideration the situation and work out a plan. It was all done in thought. I can, by a mental process, see the changed approach, the graded lawns, the enlarged veranda, the great fire-place and the towering chimneys. In thought vibrations these changes have already been made. They exist in mind, which is matter, and all that remains is to have the mental plans put upon paper and sent to the builder, who will give them physical expression, by constructing in gross matter what now exists in refined matter.

So it is in the afterlife. The home and environment are designed in thought, created in spirit matter, which is also mind, and its beauty and grandeur are only limited by the purity and progression of our earth life. They do not give their thought physical expression; they have nothing physical. Those in the other life have limitations, as we have. We differ in our creations only in the manner of expression. The one must be suitable to physical requirements, the other to spirit requirements; both are mental processes. One is expressed in gross matter, while the other consists of spirit matter and spirit expression.

The next life, in its inception, is the sum-total of this life, nothing more. And the structure fashioned by our acts and deeds here, is that which we must inhabit when we enter the spirit world.

The idea that all space is peopled and that in the universe there are no waste places, is startling, but it must appeal to our reason. The Master Mind, in creating, so planned that all space should be of use and occupied, for some purpose. The spirit world does not need our land, our waters, nor our physical atmosphere; they have their corresponding elements. Who shall say they cannot live and move in the invisible sphere about us, and surround themselves with thought creations? They live beyond and outside physical bodies, beyond our vision, yet with us. While their presence is felt by the many, it is known only by the few. This is the great misfortune of our so called civilized world.

Whatever of the spirit sphere we are prepared for when we leave the earth plane, that spiritual sphere we shall inhabit. Our homes will be such as we have made ourselves. Kindred souls mingle together there as they do upon earth, sympathizing with and enjoying the society of one another. The homes there are as varied as upon earth, but each one has its own architect.

I have never been told, and I do not comprehend, just how in this life we are actually building the homes we shall occupy in the next. Probably it is because we cannot grasp the action or product of thought, which never for one moment is inactive. Comprehension of this process will come some time.

I have never been able to make clear in my mind just the process in and by which our thoughts and acts create in the afterlife the environment that they do. Take the following description:

"One passing from the earth plane finds a home which, to his perception, is substantial, objective, familiar and real. It embodies and represents his thoughts, purposes and attainments, the outward expression of his mental, moral and spiritual self. That home is healthful, attractive, artistic and beautiful, if he has provided the requisite conditions. Whatever it is, it is home."

In this regard, it may be noted that our thoughts must, and do, find expression. A thing is thought out before it is carried out, and if those relating to the physical are built, why not others that relate to spiritual conditions? This subject is but one of many I do not as yet understand. Then, again, I wonder if I fully comprehend any matter relating to the next life.

There are many spheres in the spirit world. To some the highest spiritual life is full of activity. No such heaven will appeal, to the tired earth soul. He will long for some friendly haven of rest, and he will find it. To those in bondage, the afterlife is freedom. To the sick, it is health. To the cripple, it is strength and unlimited space in which to wander. To the tired laborer, it is eternity, a place without time and where there is no thought nor care of time. He will find that there is no more wear and tear nor fatigue for him. No matter how many journeys he may make, he will not feel tired and worn as upon earth.

Duties there must be, where many are gathered together, but they are such duties as will be one's greatest happiness to perform.

The more noble the soul, the more it feels the encumbrance of the earthly body; it is at times an uneven partnership – that of an immortal spirit and an earthly body. How often the willing spirit is unable to keep the tired body at its many tasks, and what a release when dissolution takes place and the spirit is able to ascend higher.

What one has gained and needs will be his in the spirit spheres. There is the closest love and quickest sympathy between the earth plane and the spirit world. We shall each find a different home, suited to our work. Our work now lies upon the earth plane, and it is for us to perform the duties allotted to us. We may not be able to give to the ignorant learning, nor to the hungry food, but we can inspire their spirits to nobler, better deeds, while some one else, who is able, provides food and learning. Let them feel our love and sympathy, and let them see that, even if the clouds of adversity hang low over their heads, the soul is able to ascend to higher, better spheres. It is well to know that we do not travel the stony path of life alone, to feel that, no matter how rough or dark the way may grow, we can, if we will, stretch forth the hand and feel an answering clasp – a clasp that makes the heart grow braver. The Creator seems so far away to most of us that, unless we can have the love and help of one another, we feel lonely. It will ever be impossible for the finite to grasp the infinite, but it is possible to help one another, and find, in so doing, something that gives us courage.

10

Spirit Occupations

GAIN WE COME TO a practical question: the occupation of the countless so-called dead, their daily life, and the method adopted to reach a higher development. If there be occupation, what is the average citizen qualified to do, and, in this connection, we must here consider qualifications.

It is a fact to be noted from experience that it requires years of study and close application to do anything, except hand labor, well. One who aspires to the law must now have a fairly good education, if not that of a college graduate. Then he must enter upon four years of study, followed by years of practice, before he is qualified to do good work. It is the same with the physician, and all other professions. High position is gained by years of labor. Only when fitted is one entrusted with responsibilities, and the ambitious work long and hard to qualify themselves for the positions they would occupy. This is just and proper.

Childhood is taught, youth studies, and manhood labors to qualify for the highest place which in life they may be called upon to occupy. It is a fact to be regretted that in most instances high positions are sought for the purpose of acquiring money, and the largest amount of money possible. Worldly ambitions and desires relate almost wholly to physical things. It may be said that the development of mankind, and it has been splendid, has been along physical lines, and the question may be asked, "How are men qualified to take up work, and what is the character of work in the afterlife, if there is work?"

Before taking up that question, let us remember that nothing physical passes into the spirit world. All the money and property acquired is, as we know, divided among earth people entitled thereto, and usually it is spent with all convenient speed. Litigation pertains to property, and, there being no physical property in the afterlife, the lawyer will have no practice. The physician and surgeon will have no occupation, for the reason that the physical bodies on which they practice are not there. The only ills are mental. Scientists who recognize only matter having three dimensions will not at first be qualified intelligently to work with spirit material that is so high in vibration that they know little of it.

Nature's great purpose contemplates that mankind in this life should first of all develop the spirit, refine the inner body in which the individual functions, and qualify by years of effort to meet the conditions of all mankind, for this life is but a preparatory school in nature's great plan.

How can we acquire spiritual riches? What must one do to become so developed that he may intelligently meet the new conditions and take up the work that will be required of him?

These are questions that can be answered. The answer is, play fair. In every transaction do to others as you would have others do to you. Help those who are less fortunate. Scatter words of kindness lavishly; lend a helping hand to those in need; let the thought be clean and pure; do not teach what you do not know; do not mislead; and labor to understand all natural law.

These things and such thoughts will refine and develop self and qualify one to enter into the new conditions in the life to come, without shame and without regret. Such has been my teaching from those in spirit life.

If everyone knew that here and now every act and thought was photographed in his psychic ether, and that in dissolution all became visible, some at least would hesitate. The thought that wrong can be hidden gives many courage. Thought makes character, and in the end character is visible.

What have I learned of the daily life and occupation of the living dead? One long an inhabitant of the higher plane, has said:

"We have schools here for the development of the soul of man, and to teach him his relation to mankind; to instruct him in the wonders of creation, impart to him knowledge of the inhabitants of the numerous worlds in space, to aid man, also, in experimenting in chemistry and all other branches of science, for in this life we can explore the uttermost extent of the universe. We also instruct in political economy and laws governing humanity.

We also point out conditions and means whereby to help the unprogressive and helpless portion of mankind."

Another states:

"Again, we have more advanced schools, colleges and great universities of leaning. The young, as you know, grow to maturity, and those who in earth life appear old at dissolution, having thrown off the old flesh garment, function in the fullness of maturity. There are here no old people – all are young – and age, as you use that word, depends on individual development. Earth people, as a rule, think that when they have passed through high school and universities, they are through with study. When they arrive here and appreciate that knowledge is the stepping stone of their progression, they attend our temples of learning in great things, where more advanced teachers instruct them."

Another said:

"In the spirit world, as in your world, are numerous libraries. These men and women grow intellectually. Many books are composed and written in spirit spheres, and the authors endeavor sometimes to impress their words and wisdom upon the brains of some sensitive ones upon the earth sphere. Again, a book written by one in your plane is by mental activity first created in spirit substance. It had to be before it could be clothed in physical substance by you, and we have all those books, as well as those wholly written by spirits, but none are permitted in our libraries that are not founded upon truth. It is interesting to see the vast number of spirit people thronging our libraries, studying the works of the more advanced spirits, similar to what is done in the libraries of earth."

Another said:

"We have hospitals, many of them mental hospitals, where the insane, weak and mentally deficient are treated and developed, and those who understand that work labor to restore normal conditions, for dissolution does not restore disordered minds or develop mentality.

"There are homes to build, and homes commenced on earth to finish; and they are as different as the homes of your earth. Yours are first fashioned in our ether, then constructed out of earth material by the hand of man. Ours are made out of etheric material and fashioned and erected by and through mental or, to be more correct, spirit thought. All this, as with you, requires effort. You may hire others to build earth homes, but here each builds his own, and many are very busy doing it.

"You ask me to speak particularly as to the occupation of our people. It is a subject vast in extent, for our labors transcend yours, though our methods are different. While our labor is largely in the mental or spirit field of action, yet you must remember we have fields and vegetation where those versed in such work find occupation. But it is in the more advanced field of chemistry and philosophy that spirit people seek to enter, and here millions labor to understand and comprehend the laws of Nature, and how to apply them. It is a busy world and no drones are found, except in the earthbound or lowest of the spirit spheres."

Concerning different avocations, this one said:

"I am here in this way to try to tell you of some of the conditions of our world. Here we have different avocations assigned to us, according to our needs and desires.

"Some engage in teaching and training the intellect of those who need and desire such training.

"Some with great love of children find ample opportunity for the use and enjoyment of this attribute of their natures in the kindergartens for the many thousands of children continually arriving on these shores.

"Some are most happy in endeavoring to assist the friends of earth into higher and better conditions and in counteracting the abnormal influences of undeveloped and misdirected spirits over the minds of mortals.

"So it is that there is work of benevolence and philanthropy for all who are prepared for such work.

"The exercise of active philoprogenitiveness furnishes the same delightful enjoyments to the soul over here as with you, and greater; for here we more clearly discern the far-reaching consequences of our endeavors to do good to whomsoever is in need of assistance.

Another said:

"Let me speak of the music here, of those harmonious vibrations that touch the soul, that universal appeal that is understood by all races, regardless of the languages they speak. The music of your world is crude, indeed, compared to celestial compositions and songs. Here we have harmonious vibrations, expressed in what is called music. It elevates the soul, and we devote much time to its cultivation and to instruments for its expression. It is all vibration. Many are occupied in this work. It is only now and then that our songs and our music are impressed on earth's sensations.

"We do not devote so much time to spirit matter as you do to physical matter. With you it dominates your thought. With us, matter is secondary, and spirit development dominates. It is so much more vital.

"The coming of infants unborn, babies and children, requires the attention of many. Those women who never in earth life knew the joys of motherhood, find it here and do that work. While some care for these little ones, others teach them.

Again, one said:

"In the lower spheres, when those who are held there realize that the only way to improve their condition is by helping others, and have a genuine desire to help, the way is shown.

"This question of spirit occupation is too great for special treatment. Occupation varies and is as diversified as the thoughts of men. But this you should know: there is work and a place for each new spirit. The pity of their poverty! Few have made any effort to find out what nature requires of them here; few ever gave the subject a single thought. And so they come, one by one, but with a great crowd every hour, and only now and then we find a spirit that can take up and do good work; the others have to be taught, even as little children are taught the simplest things."

Another said:

"Those who have led clean, fine lives, and have enriched the world, come here and, without a break, take up their work and go on.

"I could write a volume on the occupations of those who have preceded us, but enough has been said to impress mankind that the afterlife is real, and that there we work to develop the spirit, just as here we labor to develop and adorn the physical, while the spirit hungers and development is stayed.

What position will the average individual occupy when he enters the new life? What position has he qualified himself to fill intelligently? Stripped of all earthly possessions, money, goods and chattels gone, he has nothing left but the spirit clothed with kindly acts that have enriched his soul. If he has made the world happier and better, he goes radiant and glorious.

Ideals are like stars. We shall not succeed in touching them with our hands, but, like the traveler in the desert, we take them as our guides. Should not the young be impressed with the fact that the ideal life is one that has enriched itself spiritually, and that material wealth is in all cases a secondary consideration?

Again, one, describing conditions in the great beyond, says:

"The realities of the spirit world are beyond description. I might spend hours telling you of it and not reach your minds with any conception of its glory, its greatness, its grandeur. It is so vast in extent, so marvelous, that any attempt to give you more than a faint idea would be futile. Not until you get here and see for yourself can you have any conception of the home of the soul. We have our mission – to try to get knowledge through to the shore line of your earth. We are working our best to enlighten the world and prepare its people for the death change. It is our business to instruct those who need help, the same here as with you. Many thousands of your people cannot even read, and reach us with so limited mental development as to need all our energies in their advancement out of ignorance, wrong education and false religious teachings. Few on your earth have any idea of the changes that take place along the life line. As they come, we gather and instruct them as you do in your schools – especially in your night schools, where the ignorant seek enlightenment.

"I am impressed with the fact that very many of those called learned will realize at the end that they are among those that need teachers, and will find it necessary to attend night-school in this spirit world."

11

Poverty in the Afterlife

ONE WHO ATTEMPTS to change or modify the thoughts, ambitions and desires of mankind, is undertaking a great task. The American people, more than any other, are taught from infancy that the desired goal is wealth – material wealth – and, such is the prodigality of the times, money is necessary for the pace that is set. Money – the ring and shine of gold becomes alluring, and the ambition of each is for its accumulation. The length to which some go, and the things that some do to possess themselves of it, stagger the mind, at least of those who have a clearer vision.

It is right and very proper to provide for those dependent, in a suitable manner; but, we owe it to ourselves to provide for and enrich ourselves, both here and hereafter. Some few gather spiritual wealth that enriches beyond this earth life – the many go out into the great beyond paupers.

I am impressed to urge the importance of so living and doing that when we leave this world and also leave the material wealth that we have gathered with such great effort, we may possess a spiritual wealth of vastly more importance than stock and bonds and physical properties. This involves an awakening, a change of ideals, modified ambitions, new thoughts, new hopes, and new desires.

This spiritual wealth that becomes ours for all time, and enriches us in the great beyond, is accumulated without great effort. It is gathered simply by being fair in all our dealings, just to all men, and by helping those less fortunate than ourselves. This does not necessarily contemplate the expenditure of money, for a kind thought, a generous act, a little sympathy, an encouraging word, sets in motion vibrations in and about us that become a very part of us, refine our natures, spiritualize our souls, and better our conditions both here and hereafter.

We enrich ourselves by helping others, not by cheating or taking advantage of those with whom we have dealings. When we are unfair in a transaction, get the best of another and obtain his property, while we may do so without violating any civil law, we gain no profit, for in the end the wrong must be undone and the property returned. There is a law, taught in the dawn of civilization, that transcends the rules of modern times. It is, "Do unto others what we would have them do unto us." And eternal justice requires compensation for violation of this great law. If we build about us crude conditions, we must expect to enter into the environment which our acts and thoughts have created. This is fair; this is justice.

I do not speak from a religious standpoint. This work has nothing to do with religion of any kind. I am writing about facts and conditions, here and beyond, as I have come to know them; they are interwoven now and always have been and ever will be. Every act that we do is known here, and is visible and lives there, for we take them with us.

Take an inventory, look the situation over squarely and fairly. What have you done that will provide food, raiment and home in the Afterlife? How have you developed? The idea that here and now we can and should do and provide all those things has not been well impressed on the human mind. Would it not be the part of wisdom to give this subject a little thought, give half as much to the accumulation of spiritual as you do to material wealth, and so make happier and richer those who are now in the hereafter and ourselves and others here?

Let me quote directly from one in the next life, who has given this subject thought and who speaks from experience. This statement should create a profound impression on all thinking men and women; it is from one who actually lives and labors in that place we call the Afterlife:

"The majority of people are so intent on things material that those of a spiritual nature are either thrust into the background or forgotten altogether. This is a deplorable state of things and one which we earnestly desire to remedy.

"The mere struggle to live and provide themselves and their dependents with what they consider the necessities of life, engages many folks' attention to the exclusion of everything else. They just battle on from day to day because they must, or else become a burden to others. Such endeavor in their case is right and necessary and, if it is carried on in a brave and hopeful spirit, it is greatly to be admired.

"At the same time they would be greatly helped, and their burdens lightened considerably, if they would take time from their incessant struggle after material things to store up for themselves treasures of a spiritual nature.

"Wealth of this kind is of inestimable value and well

worth a little trouble to procure. Unlike earthly riches it makes life on the earth easier and pleasanter for its possessor and his associates, and ensures for him a happy and useful time when his earthly life ends and his spiritual existence begins.

"One who has given all or nearly all of his time and thought to material things has so much to learn on arriving here, that it is a comparatively long time before he begins to 'find' himself sufficiently to understand and enjoy the spiritual life. Such an one, if he had given more time and thought to spiritual things during his earth life, could have immediately claimed his spiritual treasures – which would have been carefully stored up for him until such time as he had need of them – and he would have been helped and his new life made much easier and pleasanter by the possession of these riches. As it is, he has to make his way, in a spiritual sense, in much the same way as a penniless wayfarer, on arriving in a new locality, must set about earning his daily bread in the material world.

"Everyone knows what a handicap the lack of capital is in your world. Well, exactly the same thing applies here. Folks arriving here in the spiritually destitute condition before mentioned have just as hard, if not a harder, struggle to make their way in the spiritual life as any one who is left without means on earth. People placed in the latter condition may and very often do receive financial help from friends and relatives, or societies which deal with that sort of thing, but there are no charitable institutions here. That is to say, no spirit ever gets something for nothing, or without effort on his part. Though we older spirits can and do help newcomers, we cannot give them spiritual riches

– we can only show them how they may acquire them for themselves.

Another spirit says:

"If newly-arrived spirits have a desire to learn how to make a spiritual living, so to speak, we can instruct them, so that in time they will become independent and will know how to set about the task of amassing wealth of a spiritual nature for themselves.

"Such wealth is not easily acquired, even here, but it is possible for any and every spirit to become possessed of it in time, if he only desires it sufficiently and is willing to work hard to get it. This may sound as if selfishness were encouraged here, but that is not so. Spirits can become possessed of the wealth here spoken of only by loving and unselfish conduct toward others. They must learn to work gladly and without thought of reward before they can hope to enjoy the fruits of their labors.

"There must be literally 'a labor of love,' and when self is utterly forgotten in a desire to help others, great and satisfying will be their reward. No goal on earth is, or ever can be, so well worth striving after. For, after all, though it is difficult to make humanity realize it fully, the things of the soul are so much more worthwhile, and infinitely more lasting, than any earthly joys and pleasures can possibly be."

So little thought has been given to the necessity of gathering spiritual wealth to enrich us beyond this physical life, so little thought has also been given to means and method, that the question may fairly be asked: How is it done?

To answer so important a question requires a little thought and some reasoning, for it is only through the avenue of reason we comprehend the intangible.

Every physical act has a physical result, every cause its legitimate effect. Advancing the spark to meet the gas, we have combustion, and the energy released is expressed in motion visible and tangible. We lay one brick upon another, embedded in plaster or cement, and we build a wall. Everyone endeavors to have a home of his own – all the result of effort, every fine spiritual act and thought changes the etheric condition about the individual. Every thought has color and is expressed in shade. Nature abhors stagnation; every hour we are improving or impoverishing our very selves; one cannot stand still.

But how can individual acts enrich us in the afterlife, you ask again? There is not one law for the spirit world and another for the physical. There is one law for both, for both blend and are really one. Simply the one is to our present eyes invisible, and the other visible, because of the different vibrations or modes of motion. Dissolution simply changes the plane of action.

We illustrate. To help another with kindly words and suggestion, to give where hunger stalks, brings joy and happiness to giver and beneficiary. Giving of material wealth is no more important than words of encouragement and tender sympathy.

The peace and comfort produced by such acts are reflected, and enrich us not only here but hereafter; charity enriches the donor more than those to whom it is given. It has been well said that the only wealth one carries into the great beyond is that he gives away here, and it will be remembered that in the next life, where money is no more, the only way one can enrich himself is by helping others. It is well to have a good start by commencing here, for the only genuine happiness we gain now is by helping others to better their condition.

We are building character every day, and, on the threshold of the Afterlife, stripped of all material wealth, we face the endless future, either rich in generous acts or paupers in a world of plenty. If mankind understood these conditions, there would be more fair dealing, less selfishness – a happier world, a richer world, a better world, and as we go one by one, we should meet the new life with the wealth of generous acts and thoughts and deeds.

Thoughts are things, and every act and thought functions around and about us in that substance called ether, sometimes called the aura. That substance, woven of the warp and woof of an act and thought, envelops us now and ever will, invisible to us now but ever visible to all in the life that follows. With this in mind, let us pause for a moment and seriously consider what kind of an etheric garment we are weaving day by day, and how our spirits will appear as we approach the Frontiers of the Afterlife. Will we go with the consciousness of a life well spent, rich with generous acts and kindly deeds, and, radiant with the soul's emanations, meet the outstretched hands and proudly reply to the words and songs of welcome? Or shall we approach this goal with soul shriveled by selfishness, lust and greed, from which no light of generous acts pierces the gloom?

I have talked with many who have gone out into darkness of their own creation, poor and alone, and long have they sought for the light that ultimately comes to all that live.

12

Child Life Beyond

DURING MY MANY years of scientific investigation I invited many men and women to
witness my work, and, among them found a
few possessing the psychic force that could be utilized
by spirit people in sending messages. I recall that Mrs.
S. was told one night that her young daughter, 12 years
of age, could do automatic writing if properly instruct-
ed. The trial was made. The child sat in an upholstered
chair, with pencil and paper, which she magnetized by
passing her hand over it for a moment, and then apparently she slept. It was a complete trance condition.
After a few trials, her hand would write with great
rapidity, and in that manner a conversation could be
carried on with spirit people with great satisfaction.
In this manner many evidential facts were obtained.
There never was the slightest doubt that spirit people
controlled her hand.

I have had similar experiences with several others,
and there is not a particle of doubt in my mind, and in
the minds of others who have witnessed such work, of
the genuineness of automatic writing.

I wish to mention Mrs. H., a lady of rare refinement
and great spirituality. I aided her development in automatic writing. She is today the most wonderful writer
that I know – absolutely reliable. I make this statement
after receiving hundreds of messages through her hand.
With her, it is spirit suggestion. She gets the messages
by dictation, knowing at the moment the word she is

writing, but not the communication as a whole until it is read afterwards. This is a most satisfactory method, second only to the direct or independent voice such as I have obtained with the aid of Emily S. French.

I mention Mrs. H. and her marvelous powers, for the reason that I am going to append a series of letters from a young boy in the spirit world, written automatically to his sorrowing mother still in earth life. I hope they will comfort thousands of other mothers who mourn for children who have gone from them. These letters were written from time to time in my presence and are authentic:

First letter
"Oh Mummie, Mummie, don't cry so. It makes me so unhappy, and I can't make you feel my arms around you. If you would only smile and be glad, I'd be quite happy, because, dear little Mummie, I see ever so many lovely people who seem to be waiting to take me some place. They are all smiling, and talking together as they wait for me to be ready to go to them. One just came to me, a darling little girl; she says she is my baby sister, you told me went to heaven; she has the loveliest face, it looks all shiny, as though there was a lamp inside her eyes. Mummie, she wants to take me home with her, but I just can't leave you:

Second letter
"Darling, I held you so tight last night, and it seemed you must have felt me, for you smiled in your sleep and said my name. When I kissed you, because you seemed happier, I went with Marian to see our home. It is a darling cottage, and every room is so interesting.

Grandma takes care of us and says the house is one she built while she lived with us; she says she did not know it at the time, but she was just as happy and good and did kind things for people, and each kind thing helped build the cottage. Some people do so much good, they have quite big houses, but they can't be any nicer than Grandma's. Hers is just filled with interesting things. She says she has lived in it and improved her mind. She said at first it was just warm and cozy, because she did not have an intellectual mind; but she has studied, and the rooms are filled with pretty things and books, and all sorts of things. When you are happier, I think I'll have a lovely time and learn a lot. Sister Marian's room is beautiful. She has lived there all her life, since a baby, and everything in her room is so beautiful and sweet.

Third letter

"Oh Mummie dear, why do you grieve so? I am well and could be happy, only your sad face keeps me wanting to be near you and comfort you. I saw Marian do such an interesting thing today. She took me to a tumble-down hut, and let me look in while she went in. There was a man in there, moaning and crying. He kept saying, 'It's so cold and dark, I can't see a thing.' Over and over he said it.

"Marian just went to him and laid her hand on his eyes, which were closed. I could see that she was thinking, without her saying a word. It was very strange, yet seemed quite all right. Marian was thinking:

'Dear man, you are just cold and alone, because when you were on earth you never thought of any one but yourself, and were so selfish and cross and horrid; but you were not happy. Don't you want to be happy?'

"And the man said: 'Yes, I want to be happy, but I can't do anything.'

Then Marian said:

"Oh dear, yes you can. Just think of some one very miserable you'd like to help." And the man said:

"Why there was my foster brother. I was so mean to him; I'm sorry, can I help him?"

"Because he said, 'I'm sorry, I want to help,' she took her hand from his eyes, and he looked around and could see. The hut that was so dark was beginning to get lighter. He began to look relieved and happier, and begged her to show him what to do, and Marian said:

"I'll take you where you can do a great deal for people. That is my business, to help people that way."

"Her face was wonderful when she said it. I think I have a splendid sister."

Fourth letter

"Mummie dear, you have made me so happy, by being cheerful. I know it will be easier all the time for you, because you will come to know that I am not miserable and only unhappy when you grieve. Some way, here in this life, things seem so much more real, and it is so easy to learn things. Grandma says we have to go on learning until we are very wise indeed, because we must try to be perfect, and we can't be that unless our minds are full of good things. I love the music – the air seems to throb with it some times, and it seems to go so deep inside of you it becomes a part of you, and afterwards you feel as if you had been having a drink of water when very thirsty, so refreshed and washed clean of everything but the nicest thoughts and feelings. There seems to be a good deal for people to do, besides learn things chiefly, helping others. The very good girls, like Marian, just show people how to begin, and then they themselves have to work and help, and, more than all, have nice thoughts. So many people do not know about it here, and I am sure if they did they would not do lots of mean things they do, because it all counts against you and you have just that much longer to work before you can do all the beautiful things there are. We sing and dance and romp, in our recreation times, and then we listen to very wise people who teach us things. I always wanted to make things up – new machines and inventions – and that is what I am going to study for. When I know how, and have worked out something new and wonderful, I am to find an inventor and be with him a lot. In time I can make him think what I am thinking; then he will make my plans. Won't that be fun?"

Fifth letter

"Darling little Mumsie, I have not talked to you for quite a long time, because I have been busy; but now that you know so much about me, and are feeling more contented, I can go on living here without worrying over you and trying to comfort you. You see, it's really just as though I was away at school, and at first one is always homesick; but now we can look forward to a vacation time when you will come to me and we shall be together always, and I shall have such heaps of things to tell you and show you. There is no wasted time here; waste means ignorance, and ignorance is almost wicked, because we should progress a little each day – that is one of our laws. We have to study these laws. I will try and tell you as well as I can some of them. In the first place, we must know what is good, and by knowing that, all the other laws follow easily. When we know good, we know that right follows, and then love and harmony and knowledge and power, and then progress follows as naturally as a flower grows in the sun. You will think this sounds queer from your little boy, that I have changed a lot; but I haven't so much, Mummie – I have just grown to understand the real things in life, what we all have felt inside of us always."

Sixth letter

"Dear Mummie, I am learning many things that are necessary in this life, now you are so much happier about me and feel so sure that everything is all right with me. It used to scare me, when I saw any one who had died; or, when I thought of being put in the cemetery, it seemed awful – so lonely and strange; but now I know how different it is and wish every boy knew that dying is just like getting a new suit and discarding the old. The real you inside the new feels just the same, only we have to learn to think differently about most things. I mean, we must change some of our ideas, but the new ones are much nicer and make living here easier. I wish every one knew this before he came here and then no one would fear, and everything would be so nice and comfy.

"Marian and I came to you on Christmas morning and kissed your dear face; you must have felt all our love and happiness. We will come to you like that often, and some day you will come and live with us; then you will learn so many lovely things we cannot some way seem to tell you. There are such nice people always with us, and you will love it just as we do, Grandma says she is happy to have me with her, and to tell you that she, with the help of friends and teachers, will bring me up to manhood and that you will be proud of me when you come.

"Your own little boy."

Another spirit mother described child life, as follows:

"I will tell you about the home for little children first of all. No mother who loses a wee one need grieve, because she thinks the dear mite will have no one to love it and to soothe its small fears and worries. You would love to see all the happy wee things we have here, some of whom had a very sad time during their brief sojourn on earth. Not one single baby, out of all the millions which come here, ever lacks mothering. They are surrounded by an atmosphere of love and just grow and blossom, as a result of these happy conditions, like so many rare and beautiful flowers. The place where they are rings with the sound of their happy laughter; there is no pain or sorrow for them here and they have no cause for tears. They romp and play and do all manner of things which delight the heart of a child.

"They are free to enjoy every moment, and they do. There are no quarrels or sulks to mar their happy times together; their bright faces and sweet presences are a constant delight, especially to those folks who have always loved children. The men and women who were denied children on earth, and had always longed for them, are in their element when they come over and are free to lavish all their love for children on these darlings. The children grow up in time, as they would on earth, but they are free from sin. They can, therefore, go right on helping the spirits of those who spent many years on earth and are not free from the effects of sin. These spirits need help and guidance.

"I will now tell you about the place where the children come to grow up. It is a wonderful place and there are all sorts of lovely things they can do. The very tiny ones cannot play with the older ones any more than they can on earth. They just need loving arms around them and soft voices to soothe them. They get these always. There are always plenty of 'mother spirits' to look after the wee ones. It is the work they love and are best fitted for. We are all given the work we like best and are most capable of doing.

"As we progress some of us are able to undertake more and more difficult tasks, and that phrase about 'the joy being in the doing, not the task that is done,' is very true here. Most of us find a great joy in our work. I will tell you something about the doings of the older children. The toddlers are such darlings and would rejoice any mother's heart. Their faces are so bright and happy and they are so full of life, and bubble over with fun. There are no sad, wistful little faces here, as you often see on earth – caused by lack of love, the sins of their parents, and other things. These fortunate little ones have a delightful time. They run and dance and sing and jump for sheer joy. They paddle in crystal streams and build castles on lovely beaches, where the sand is like pure gold and the water is like myriads of gems.

"There are beautiful grassy places for them to play on, where they can run races and play all the games which children love. There are also exquisite fern groves, where every kind of beautiful fern flourishes, and dainty little streams tinkle gaily along, joining, it seems, in the children's merriment. There are so many beautiful and wonderful and delightful things in this enormous 'children's playground' that you will not have time to write down descriptions of half its beauties."

13

Earthbound

THERE WERE FEW nights during the years of scientific investigation that I did not talk with earthbound spirit people, usually with several, and I have learned much of their condition.

"What creates the earthbound condition?" is the first question properly asked. I answer, as I have been answered thousands of times:

"The lives they led, and the conditions they created for themselves, for as a man sows so shall he reap.

"The laws of nature, the laws under which we live, are not only fixed and definite, but eternally just.

Thoughts are things, and every moment as they emanate from each individual something is added to his character. It is enriched or impoverished, and if no light emanates from it one is held at his dissolution within the lower planes that circle this globe. The selfish character, like the miser in the "Chimes of Normandy," the cruel, the immoral and wanton, the thief, the murderer – is it not just that they be herded together until they have lived over each wrong act, lived it aright and made compensation, thus qualifying themselves for association with a finer group? The justice that meets human souls at the frontier is complete. They enter into a condition which is of their own creation. They find such light as they radiate, and no more. There is no escape in the afterlife from the consequences of things done and performed in this. In this plane, so close about the earth that in reality it is a part of it, the wicked, the malicious and base, and all those who have acquired no spiritual development, are held. This plane has various stages. Some are in total darkness, some in half light; all in all, it is at most a twilight zone between the spiritual and physical worlds. Here old appetites, thoughts and desires hold sway as before. In this zone a great mass of undeveloped people of the same general character, with a desire for spirituality no greater than when living in the physical body, remain. Their condition is much worse than in this world, for there is not the opportunity for reformation that there was before. There the great law of attraction holds together those of a similar character, so that these live in mental poverty until they have a desire for better things. Then the way is shown and they work slowly out by their own efforts, but the labor is long and the path dim that leads to the zones of happiness and peace. Bruno said:

"Whatever good a man has to his credit, whether it be much or little, is the seed from which he grows eternally.

"In my talks with earthbound spirit people I never found two exactly alike, any more than they can be found alike here. That change did not alter or improve them. This is evidently Hell, so much talked of and feared. I recall so many earthbound that have told of the horror of their condition, that it is with difficulty I choose specific individuals, for I had speech with: such a great number. It is like seeing the paintings in the principal galleries of Europe. There are many, but some stand out prominently. This is the story told by one:

"I was not a good man among men. I was selfish, cruel, took human life, and was, as I now know, killed while committing a crime. When I awoke it was very dark, and, not knowing what had happened, I called in anger, but my companions did not come. My voice echoed back to me again and again, and I began to think I was in a cave. I arose and groped about in the darkness, but I could not find the walls, though I walked for hours. I did not feel hunger or thirst, and days and months passed, while I was ever searching for the walls that threw back the echo of my call. Can you imagine the sensation that you would have, to be lost in an open forest with the sun in the sky, to say nothing of being lost in darkness? My sensations and suffering beggar description.

"After a very long time I saw a light, and as it approached I saw that it shone or radiated from the form of a man. 'My brother,' the man said, 'you are in spiritual darkness; how can I help you?' He came and, putting forth his hands, would have touched me, but I was speechless and rushed away in fear. Thereafter when I saw a light I would hide, fearing I would be arrested, for at that time I did not know I had left my physical body. I became desperate, and the next time a light approached I waited. Coming to me, a man from whose body light radiated, as before, said, 'What do you wish?' I replied, 'I want to get out of this prison.' 'You are not in prison; you are dead.' I cursed him for making such foolish statements, and he was gone.

"Again I was alone in darkness. How long this continued I know not, for, there being no day, I could not count time. Again there came one to me and again I demanded that I be released from my prison. He calmly and kindly replied, 'You are not in prison; you are a spirit.' That seemed to me the height of absurdity, for I was very much alive; but I listened and he told me that I 'had made the change' and brought another, an artist, who drew pictures of my youth and the faces of my boyhood friends, and, one by one sketched those acts and deeds and wrongs that I had done. Then the light faded and they were gone and I was left alone to think." When I had fully come to appreciate my condition and to regret the wrong done and the suffering caused by me, there came a desire to do what I could to make reparation. Then came other spirit people to encourage me and suggest what I must do to obtain spiritual growth and with it, the light. Not one offered to take my burden, or to undo the wrong that I had done; that was for me; they only pointed out the way. I was told there were none to forgive me, except the injured; no savior but himself.

"Step by step I went forward; hour by hour I made reparation and lived again each wrong and lived it right; and day by day, as you count time, I undid my wrong and added to the right. The way was long, the labor intense, but in it I found a happiness I had never known before. For I was building my character; the atom of good was striving for its spirituality. Now that is all behind me, and I live in the glorious and effulgent light of the spirit world, laboring among congenial souls. I was seared by the fire of selfishness and wrong doing. I paid, and paid to the last farthing, the penalty. Now I am at peace with the spirit world, as it is with me.

"I send this message back to the world of men: 'There is not in the universe a method by which any one can escape the penalty of wrong.' Had I known this fact, I would have lived among you honestly and been fair with my fellow men. I did not know it, and

I have paid in full, as all will pay in full, for ignorance will not excuse.

"It has been a privilege to tell through you of my experience in the earthbound zone of the spirit world. If one man will hesitate when contemplating a single selfish or wrong act, and turn from it because of better understanding, it will reflect upon me and better my condition."

The following statement as to earthbound conditions is from another spirit:

"The belts or zones that lie close around your earth are designed for the habitation of undeveloped spirits when out of the body; as they outgrow the passions of earth and become more refined, they pass to another or higher zone. Many remain in the first or earth zone for years.

"We of the higher zones try to teach them that they must forgive and forget the wrongs of earth and in that work, advance out of the earthbound condition, but many turn a deaf ear to our suggestions and try to revenge the wrong done to them when on earth; all this is intensely human, and this zone, so like the physical, is very real.

"Those who have progressed, those who in the beginning passed directly through this belt, because of their spirituality, would never come back into that atmosphere, were it not for their love for and desire to help humanity.

In explanation of this condition another spirit said:

"Many on leaving the mortal body are still in earthly conditions, found on the grosser spiritual side you call the lower sphere, where the spiritual senses are not yet awakened to susceptibility of spiritual discernment."

Again, one said:

"I find a great many come from earth life in a very darkened condition; and, of course, they gravitate or are drawn to localities of corresponding conditions. They don't know just where they ought to go or what to do. In fact, many are ignorant of any other than the condition in which they find themselves. Many, too many, are in a condition of slumbering, some in a "deep sleep which lasts a long time, and great effort is put forth to awake such spirit people.

This is the experience of another spirit:

"I had been in the afterlife a number of years when I was taken into the lowest sphere, and what I saw has lingered in my memory ever since. I was taken by a guide accustomed to work in the earthbound plane. We move, as you know, with the rapidity of thought. My first impression was of a descent in the dark, all about me gloom, and to add to the horror I could hear voices though I could not see any one. After a time, when as it seemed, I grew accustomed to the darkness, I could see people about me, poor men and women who did not realize they had left the physical body – some shrieking because they could not escape their victims; those they had wronged were not there, it was their awakening consciousness that brought such vision. The guide spoke gently to them. Some answered with coarse jests, others with mirthless laughter; but a few came close and listened while he told them of their condition and what must be done to work out of this darkness, which was of their own creation. We have as much trouble in making these poor spirit people understand conditions beyond their sight and touch, as you have with earth people.

"In the beginning when I talked with spirits who did not know they were dead, as that word is commonly used, it staggered my thought. I could not then conceive that one could be in that condition and not know it. I did not then know that the next life was so material, so tangible, and, in the lower spheres, so like our own; neither did I know that here and now we possess an inner body, which, when separated from the outer flesh garment, is identically the same as before, with the same feature, expression and thoughts. With the first or lower sphere actually blending with our world as it does, how can those who have just gone understand their condition, if they possess no knowledge concerning this change?

In the presence of such known facts, the question of the continuity of life no longer remains, and we advance to the more important proposition of what are the conditions the so-called dead meet when they cross the border. Where is the border? Where is the afterlife and what is the new environment? These questions are vital and are being answered from day to day, though few ask the question, and of those who do ask, a lesser number understand. The world is too busy getting money to give this subject serious thought.

Let it not be understood that all the living dead are earthbound and held in such zone of darkness; of all that go, only a few of the many are there held. But let it be remembered that conditions in spirit planes vary as the varying characters of men, and that each reaches that environment for which his earth life has fitted him. There he will live until by growth be has earned a more advanced zone.

The experiences of these spirits were unusual,

terrible in severity, and possibly extreme, but they are necessary to illustrate what the degenerate and wicked must expect. Others have told of the wonders and delights of the next conditions, as they were enabled to feel and visualize them in the beginning. Where spirit people are, what they see and enjoy, depends on just what their earth life earned. How many know this fact?

The fortunate should help the unfortunate; the strong should defend the weak; the intellectual should lead with gentle hands the mental poor. This is the highest conception of religion in both worlds, and a necessary process if we would enrich ourselves in either.

A spirit has said:

"You can have no idea of the nature and extent of punishment which some spirits have to undergo. There is no hell, nor is torture inflicted in the spirit world. Every one that comes brings the punishment with him in his own nature. When a spirit passes from the earth to this world, every trait of his natural habits, principles and passions is delineated on his spirit features. There can be no deceptions with us. You will be placed with those of similar character, whose natures correspond with yours.

"There is no night here, and consequently no day, at least not as I once measured, and as you still measure time. Time here is measured only by emotions, events and deeds. There are dark places and darker souls, as there are on earth."

14

Helping the Dead

I N MY EARLY WORK I was told much that baffled understanding. Things which now appear simple, then seemed impossible. The statement that there were many in the afterlife who did not know that they had made the great change and were out of their physical bodies, was beyond my comprehension, though many whom I identified so stated.

At this period of my work I had the usual indefinite, hazy notion that Heaven, so-called, was far away, that something survived dissolution, but what it was I had never been able even to define, any more than the average Christian can define it today. I did not then know that this inner body at dissolution advanced to material spirit zones that encircle this earth, and that those whose spirituality did not carry them into the higher spheres did not for a long time get beyond the earthbound plane, and that many were able to go in and out of our homes and offices as before, though they could not make us answer them or realize their presence.

Some are in such a state that the helpers in the higher life cannot reach them, and it is only by uniting our forces and working together that these poor, souls are brought to consciousness and shown how they can develop and progress. Those earthbound ones are the spirit people who need our help.

When I state that one-half of each of the evenings – during all the years of my work was devoted, with the help of the spirit group working with me, to helping this class of spirits, one may get an idea of the great necessity for it.

Bear in mind that Mrs. French, the psychic in whose presence this work was done, did not do the talking. She was not in a trance, but contributed psychic force necessary in our work. Bear in mind, again, that, when out of the physical housing, spirit people have vocal and respiratory organs as in earth life, and can speak as before, being heard by mortal ear when conditions are as I learned to make them.

Usually some learned spirit spoke on some phase or condition of the next life, which discourse, at such times as I was able to procure the services of a stenographer who could write in the dark, was taken in shorthand. Then came what we called our "Mission Work.

"Thousands upon thousands of spirit people spoke in this work and never any two in the same condition or with similar ideas or experiences, for they were different as in this life. Many were awakened apparently after long periods of time; others were in darkness, and could not find the light; others did not realize that they had left the old earth body; others knew they had, but found nothing as they expected. Some had a craving for liquor and a desire to satisfy old appetites; while others came for suggestions and advancement. The procession was endless and the need beyond description.

Those who are advanced in the afterlife are ever ready and anxious to help any below them, and they do a wonderful work. But there are many whom they can not reach, and it is only by blending their forces with ours that a condition was created where these poor souls could be brought to a realization of their condition and started toward a higher development.

Spirit people are not infinite; they are limited in their sphere, as we are in ours, and so, for twenty-two years, we worked together to help earthbound spirits. It was the most important work I ever did, beside which all my professional achievements sink into obscurity and are as nothing. This was a real pleasure and a great privilege. Let me illustrate the character of this work.

I was in my own home one evening, alone with Mrs. French. A storm had passed and there could be heard the low moaning wind in the great trees outside. It was absolutely dark in the room where we sat facing each other with only a small table between us. The discourse on the scientific aspect of the next state was finished; then came silence and expectancy.

"I have wandered, for years, searching, searching, searching," a voice distressed and low, came out of the darkness; "and traveled, traveled, traveled; and I have found nothing but vegetation, and I am so weary." Then this benighted spirit apparently realized that I was visible, and he seemed to turn toward me, and said: "I don't understand. I am seeking my Savior;

I was told He would meet me, but I can't find Him, and I am lost."

I replied: "No man is ever lost." He replied: "I will be lost, if I don't find my Savior. I have searched so long!"

"Did it ever occur to you that you have no Savior but yourself?" I asked. "That cannot be," he said. "All my earth life I relied on Him to save me, and I must find Him."

"Would it not be better to try to save yourself," I said.

"No man can be saved except he believe in Christ," he answered. "We have no Savior but ourselves, and until we understand that fact and help ourselves and others, we don't find a very desirable afterlife. How do you account for the fact that you have traveled so far, met no people, and seen nothing but vegetation?" I asked.

"I don't know; I don't understand," he answered." I know and I understand," another spirit voice answered. "This man lived a narrow, selfish Christian life, simply relying on the Bible teachings, believing that the Savior would carry his burden and lead him to the great white throne, and when he realized he had passed the portal of death his first thought was to find that Savior that he had been taught to depend upon. This idea became an obsession and he started traveling with only one thought in mind. So intent was he, so centered was his thought, he saw nothing of the people or the wonders of the sphere in which he had advanced. He could not find what he sought, and he could not see or sense what he was not seeking. His journey will not end until he realizes that he is his own savior."

"That is a new idea. Who is that man?" he asked.

"A spirit like yourself," I answered.

"Is what he said true?" he asked.

"Has it not occurred to you in all this time, that, if your teaching were true, your Savior would have met you, and has not the fact that you were not so met, caused you to question your belief?" I said in reply.

"It has not before, but let me think. Have I been wrong in my belief? When I came over and failed to find Him, I should have questioned; but I did not. I thought I must search and I have searched so long," be said.

I had learned that when a spirit was really awakened

in the condition we had created where the earth and spirit spheres blend together, friends could come and help. I asked: "Don't you want to stop traveling, and see some of your family or friends?"

"I certainly do. – If I am wrong and have been wasting my life, I should like to know it," he replied.

"Look," I said: "It is growing light. How beautiful! See great throngs of people."

He said, "They are coming toward me, men and women, dead men and women, but they don't look dead. They appear just as they did before, and so do I. There comes a friend who beckons me. May I go?"

"Yes," I answered. "The thought that dominated you is broken and now you are free. Go with those who have come to help you, and they will show you how to help yourself."

He was gone, then silence again, the night wind and the darkness; while in the room tiny non-luminous points of light appeared, and substance like faint clouds in a summer sky floated and visibly formed into indefinite shapes, as the spirit chemist restored conditions to the psychic normal. Again the stress and the expectant speech. We could always feel the effort that was apparently necessary to clothe with ectoplasm a spirit's vocal organs, so that its voice would sound in our atmosphere." What are you trying to do?" another voice spoke. "I have been watching these manipulations with great interest; a gentleman told me to ask and I am curious."

"This lady and myself," I replied, "come together each week and with spirit aid create a condition where we can talk, voice to voice, with dead people:,

"That is positively a most absurd statement. The

dead can't talk," he said.

"Do you know that to be a fact?" I asked. "No," he answered, "I don't know it to be a fact, but if it were possible, I should have heard of it."

"Have you ever heard of obtaining messages from departed spirit people?" I asked. "Yes," be said, "I have heard such claims, but never for a moment did I consider it worthy of the slightest consideration." Did you ever really consider what would happen to you in the death change?" I asked. "No, that was a subject I did not care to think about. I have the cares of my business, which are enough," he replied.

"Stop and think for a moment; where are you now?" I said.

"I don't know; this is not my office and the surroundings are strange. I don't quite comprehend this most unusual situation. Nor do I recognize you or this lady," he answered.

"Do you recall your name and recent events?" I asked.

"Certainly," he replied, "my name is . . . my office . . . and, as I recall, I had just concluded an important conference; but this is neither my office nor my home. Where am I and how did I get here, and who are you? I have no recollection of meeting you or leaving my place of business."

"I am Mr. Randall, and you are in my home in Buffalo, and this lady and myself, with the aid of a spirit group, talk at times with those who have left the physical body, just as we are now talking to you," I replied.

"I don't understand why you speak to me in that manner. I am not dead," he said.

"Look at your body," I said.

"I am looking at it. I see no change," he answered.

"Look again. Hold up your hand to the light," I said. "My God! What has happened? My whole body is natural but it is transparent. I can see through it. What does this mean?" he asked.

"Does it not dawn on you what we are trying to convey? Recall your last sensation," I said.

"I am," he replied. "I was in my office – a feeling of great weakness came over me. I had a sensation of falling, and I don't recall anything more, until I found myself here. Do you intend to convey the suggestion that I am dead?. Is that what this talk leads to?"

"There is no death, there are no dead," I answered. "There is only change. In dissolution the inner body, released from the flesh housing, passes to the next or spirit plane, which is as material and natural as the earth life, and so similar that in the beginning many don't realize it any more than you do, and I am inclined to believe from this talk that you never developed your better self to any degree, for which reason you don't understand what is actually being done now, nor the condition in which you find yourself."

"Can it be," he replied, "that death comes without our knowing it, and that we continue to live in a world similar to that of the earth? It is a most astounding proposition. Have I really ceased to live the earth life?"

"I should infer from your statements," I answered, "that you passed out of the body suddenly, possibly with a stroke of apoplexy. What is the date?"

"This is January 20th," he replied.

"No," I answered. "It is April, and for three months you have been unconscious."

"The suggestion stirs me beyond expression," he said. "Let me think. I was in good bodily health, as I thought, engrossed in business affairs, and the idea that death would come to me never was seriously considered, and now you tell me it has overtaken me, and that I am no more of earth, and that as a spirit I can actually talk to you still in the old life. I want to think it over – I am not fully satisfied. It would seem to me if I was a spirit I would meet other spirit people. Why don't I?"

"Look about you again," I said. "While we have been talking, possibly you have not noticed what has taken place."

"Why it is growing more light, and I can see about me many I thought dead and gone," he said;

"And they tell me they have come to help me out of darkness, teach me the laws that control in this sphere of life, and point out the method by which I can develop my spirit, which I have so long neglected. This thought and their presence overwhelms me, and I must have time to realize it all."

"You have been awakened," I said, "and put in touch with those who will help you. Go with them and all will be well with you."

"Good night," he said. "I thank you.

These cases illustrate the condition in which some spirit people find themselves, the method employed in bringing them to a realization of the change that has taken place, and something of the results obtained in this mission work. Volumes could be written from the records obtained, which would further show the urgent need of work of this character.

15

Mission Work Again

A MONG THE MANY thousand cases that I In came into our mission work, some teaching great lessons stand out prominently. There lived in my home city a few years ago a man of great wealth. He had reached the age of four-score and ten, was of unimpeachable character and at the head of some of our largest financial institutions, but he was close in money matters, very close, and saved the pennies as well as the dollars. I knew him intimately, for I had an office for some years in the same building and saw him frequently. He was counted a good citizen, but not much given to relieving distress – such was the public estimation of his character.

The day came when he passed from the world of men, and was soon forgotten. Five years elapsed, during which period I went on with my work, helping those whom my co-workers brought, regardless of who or what they were, for in the democracy of death wealth and worldly distinction are lost, and only character survives.

I recall vividly the evening I shall describe, for it taught one of the greatest lessons I have ever had from this source. This night I was not alone with Mrs. French; I had as a guest Louis P. Kirchmeyer, who had psychic sight and could actually see spirit people before they spoke, as could Mrs. French. If a spirit was personally known, either could call him by name, and if I knew him well, I could usually recognize his voice.

This condition made identity in such cases beyond question.

Again, this chapel in my home where my work was carried on, with the non-luminous ribbon of light above our heads, indicated that conditions were favorable. There was never a night when we knew who would come or what we should be called upon to do, as much depended on our mental and physical condition, and then atmospheric conditions had to be considered. I seldom asked for any particular individual – ours was a scientific work, and those who needed help were brought in after the lecture, usually.

"It is so cold and dark," a voice came out of the darkness. Mr. Kirchmeyer and Mrs. French both psychically saw and recognized the gentleman mentioned above, and told me his name. After he spoke, I recognized his voice, which was somewhat peculiar. I had a high regard for this man, and, considering the lapse of five years since his passing on, was startled by what he said.

"Mr. W," I said, "I am surprised after this lapse of years to hear you make such a statement. Tell me more of your condition."

"There is around and about me a wall of money, nothing but money; it shuts out the light. It is so dark, and wherever I go I cannot get away from it, around it or over it," he replied.

"This man," said one of the spirit group who was helping in the work, "spent his whole life in accumulating money. It dominated his whole thought, it was all he built, and in coming into this life he found only the condition he had created, and, never having developed his spirit, he sheds no light on his pathway.

"Having from experience learned how to help in such cases by suggestion, I said, "Mr. W, I think you can see light if you will look. What do you see?"

"It is coming," he said, "just a ray, but wait, I see a highway leading away in the distance."

"And what do you see on that highway?" I asked.

"Nothing," he answered, "not a living thing."

"Look again," I replied.

"Yes," he said, "I now see sign boards along the sides as far as the eye will reach."

"And what, if anything, is printed on those sign boards?" I asked.

"I can only read on the first one the word 'charity.' What does it mean?" he said.

"I will tell him what it means," the same spirit who had spoken before answered. "This man never thought of charity, which is the helping of others, either by kindly words or by material aid, so with all his millions of money he came into this world a spiritual pauper. He has now found the light, will realize his misspent life, and must learn what charity is. When he has practiced it, he can read the second, sign. That highway is his to travel; it is long, but it will ultimately lead him to happiness and to a wealth he has never known."

This experience teaches us that we owe something to our fellow men, and that the more we have the more we owe to those less fortunate.

The following incident occurred on another night, and illustrates that all who pass out are not earthbound; in fact, the great majority pass at once to a higher spiritual plane and more comprehensive life. All find just what they make for themselves, be it good or bad, and enter into the particular condition for which they are fitted. The power of money is no more; the only wealth carried beyond is that given away here.

"My years have gone swiftly," another said, "since my earth friends said farewell, and I journeyed on. I was glad to make the change for myself, but regretted I could not make those left behind understand that I was not dead and that it was for my good that I stepped out of the tenement of clay and put on the garb of the immortals. I realized at once that I was out of the body, but I stayed about the home for some days before I was taken away, when I took up the work of helping those in the lower spheres. I have been familiar with your work for a long time, and am permitted to bring a soul that you can help. When his vocal organs are clothed, he will speak:

"I understand fully," another spirit said, "that I have left my physical body. I was fully conscious when the change was taking place. My first thought was that I did not want a post-mortem of my earth body, and I was relieved when I knew it was not to be done. This is a beautiful world, in which I live, with opportunities beyond your conception. When earth conditions do not bind me, I can attend great lectures, and in temples of music hear celestial song. But I am bound to earth by the sorrow of my father and mother. They brood and weep, and sorrow – for me as one dead, and that holds me like bands of steel, so that I can only at times do what other boys do. They don't understand that I am more alive than ever before, but until they give me happier thoughts my progression is stayed and I am as unhappy as they are. And I could be so happy and accomplish so much, if they would let me go. Won't you go and tell them what I have said, and change their thoughts? Tell them that death is life boundless and endless, and our sphere is filled with happiness. Please promise." I did promise, and I did go and do what I could, but human nature loves to sorrow for the so-called dead.

How miraculous, how marvelous, you say, is this work. Not at all, it is no more marvelous than what you observe from day to day, and to which you give little thought. You plant a tiny seed in the dark ground, and in a little time you see a plant full of beautiful blossoms. You plant a kernel of corn and see grain reproduced. You note the reproduction of man himself. Do you suppose that the laws, which do all these most mysterious things, are not able to clothe temporarily a spirit body so that he can speak and be heard by mortal man?

I remember how stubborn I was in the beginning of my psychic investigation. For a long time I would not admit to myself, much less to the public, the conviction that was growing within me. I had not the capacity to comprehend these simple truths. Everyone who walks in the woodland, stands by the sea, reads a book, looks at a picture, or hears a lecture, gets all the intellectual wealth he is capable of receiving, and no more.

16

Spirit Influence

HAVE SPIRIT PEOPLE any influence or control over our thought or action, if so, to what extent and by what process?

To bring ourselves intelligently to the question, we must appreciate, as we have never done before, that those out of the physical body are people, as they were before dissolution; that they live and inhabit material belts or zones about the earth; that they walk upon the city's streets; go into and out of homes, as freely as before; and are silent witnesses of our daily thought and action. They travel at will along the old highways, stay about the homes they built, see us and know our daily rants, desires and ambitions, and are familiar with the discords, as well as the harmonies, of our lives. Many become co-workers with us. I know the limitations of the human mind and its inability to grasp this simple proposition, more important than the accumulation of wealth, and I wish for many tongues that I might speak in all of nature's dialects and languages. If this fact could be brought home to all the men and women who inhabit this globe, it would revolutionize the conduct of mankind and enrich the world.

There are some truths that cannot be told too often; there are truths that, no matter how often told, seem to make no impression; there are some soils which, regardless of how perfect the seed or how thickly sown, give little return; and so, in many ways, we tell over and over again what follows dissolution, finding now and then a fertile brain.

All knowledge is the result of suggestion, which may be divided into three classes – physical, mental and spiritual. Physical suggestion is objective. Everything we see or hear in nature makes its impression on our minds. Something is by that process suggested to our senses, and, to the extent that we grasp and understand, we make it our own and thereby increase the sum-total of our knowledge. One in spirit life, who has given many lectures, said on this subject:

"Come with me through the walks of life, and see the manner of men we can help. It is not the arrogant fool who says in his heart, 'My way is the only way,' nor yet the man who weakly fears to trust his own instinct and vacillates falteringly between the opinions of man; but it is the sane, quiet thinker, who is willing to listen to all arguments and to choose wisely those that appeal alike to his heart and brain. Such we can assist by spirit-suggestion. Without his being conscious of it, we can often guide his thought along the right lines, because he is fair-minded.

"Suggestion is one of the strong factors in the life force. As you said this morning, all things have their power of suggestion. Does not a low saloon throw out its vile suggestion to all men? Whether this emanation entices or repels, depends upon the man, but its surrounding influence is felt strongly, and the suggestion is evil. A beautiful rural scene is helpful, with its suggestion of peace and harmonious coloring. And so it is through all phases of life. Hence all should seek the best, and unconsciously all do aspire to it."

Mental suggestion is the deduction or reasoning from one known cause to its effect, by which something more is suggested. By this method we prove to ourselves facts previously unknown. An illustration of deductive reasoning occurs when we accept the contention that "nothing in nature can be destroyed." From this accepted hypothesis, positing that the mind is a part of nature, just as much as the earth itself, though more important, we reason that the Master Mind which created all things has not planned the annihilation of its higher forms and preserved the lower. To do so would be both unreasonable and unjust, and in nature there is no injustice nor unreason. Man has proved that it is impossible to destroy an atom. We assert, therefore, by the process of deductive reasoning, which is really the most purely mental form of demonstration, that a human soul cannot be annihilated. It follows, by laws as certain as those pertaining to the physical, that no spirit of man has ever been destroyed. This we know, also inductively, because in company with many others who understand the elementary laws of vibration, we have talked with those who have survived the supposed destruction of death. The inductive method, then, will help to confirm the conclusions of the deductive on the subject. We know by experiment that it is possible for earth dwellers to communicate with those who have left the earth. Franklin was able to demonstrate the two methods; inductively he showed that lightning and electricity are identical, and, deductively, that houses may be protected by lightning rods. Vice versa, then, if spirit can be seen by induction to be identical with mind, deduction will enable us to conclude that spirits, still in the flesh, can have direct relations with spirits out of the flesh.

Spiritual suggestion is the method of the afterlife.

With spirit people, thought is such a positive force, and takes such definite form and shape, that it is visible. Their language is a thought language and is as well understood among them as words are among us. They soon lose all desire for physical touch or expression, finding the purely mental so much more intense; and, as they move in and out among the people of earth and see when and where they can do good, they, by a purely mental process, suggest to us often what to do and what not to do. Thus the suggestion of those who have passed out of earth life comes to us as a moral guide, whose true origin many ignore because they have absolutely no knowledge of what happens after dissolution. This form of suggestion we call intuition, impulse, or inspiration.

Spirit suggestion comes through our sub-conscious brain. Mind, whether in or beyond the physical, is a positive force in nature. Spirit people, desiring to influence our conduct to some desired end, retard their mental vibrations, and, at the same time, ours increase until our vibrations and theirs pulsate more or less in harmony; then it is possible for them to make their thought our thought, and when we, guided by their suggestion, do some good deed with their cooperation, we increase in some, degrees the sum of Universal Good. But, because those beyond the physical are not always spiritual, some being, on the contrary, of a low order of mentality and often depraved, with low instincts and base appetites, as when in the body, they, if our thoughts and desires are of a similar character, can reach our sub-conscious brains, and suggest that which will satisfy their desires. The results are base actions produced by both them and us. Man is not a mere automaton, but a personality, deriving his progression from suggestions of people both in and out of the body; and it is difficult, so subtle is spirit suggestion – to tell with any certainty whether the thought that preceded the act was one's own conception or that of some spirit working through one's brain to do good or to satisfy his own selfish desires. For this reason, one should weigh well what he has an impulse or desire to do. Good always precedes evil. First impressions are better than those which follow, because they are more spiritual.

The whole process of thought is the result of suggestion, without which ideas could be neither formulated nor expressed. Knowledge would be suppressed and evolution impossible, were it not for suggestion. The influence of the spirit world is far greater than any mortal can comprehend, because we are unable, so faint is the line of demarcation, to tell the origin, or source, of any thought.

In formulating this philosophy, I am unable to say to what extent intelligences beyond the physical have influenced my mind. My brain may have been, so to speak, a conduit of thought, and my hand an instrument to give physical expression to natural laws not at present generally understood by man. I cannot tell; I have not been conscious of any suggestions; but knowing from my conversations with spirit-people, I would not say that they have not had a very great influence in shaping this work.

I have the greatest respect and love for many who have, voice to voice, proved their identity, and given me their knowledge. What they have taught I know to just what extent they can influence our daily conduct and thought, depends on their mental conditions and ours. It is, therefore, largely an unknown influence, but an important one, which all should understand. The life of spirits is intensely active and real; they have their work along those lines for which their experience in earth life has best fitted them; they labor where there is the greatest need, where most good can be done. The ignorance of those in the physical world on this subject is very great and, as a result, their condition is so inferior to what it might be, that spirit people, realizing the deplorable situation, spend much time on the earth plane, striving to enlighten mankind and to make them live better individual lives, a task which impedes their own progress.

I recall listening, not many years ago, to a boy not more than fourteen years old, playing a great masterpiece on a violin, with marvelous technical skill. His intellect was not above the average, nor had he received any special artistic training, yet he could execute the most difficult music. One of our standard law books, recognized as an authority, was written by a boy while at college. Fiske wrote philosophy in his teens. We have always had prodigies who were able without much education, to accomplish great things. But there is nothing remarkable in this, after all; it means only that a master in spirit is able either to suggest or to work through their subconscious brains.

In some instances, like the boy violinist and Blind Tom, spirits take actual possession of the body and brain, which, for the time being, are used by them as an instrument to give physical expression to their attainments.

What is true of the boy, is true likewise of the man.

It is difficult, so great is the power of spirit minds, so fine is the line of demarcation between self and their suggestion, to tell, at all times, what is self and what is suggestion. This mind of ours is like a stream having its source among the hills and flowing toward the sea. A thought from the right finds its way to the channel; another one comes from the left and joins the current, adding volume and character; and when the stream reaches the sea of expression, it is hard to say how much of it came from the original source, how much is our own, or how much flowed in from surrounding conditions.

We hear a voice calling our name; we turn and listen; it suggests that someone would speak to us. We hesitate while the thought finds lodgment in the brain; and it, too, sets in action a line of reasoning. That thought may have been generated by a process of reasoning, and, again, it may have been the suggestion of some spirit interested in our welfare. Spirits can call as well as those in the physical body. Both can be heard, the first by the mind itself, and the latter by the physical sense of hearing. And it is difficult for any one to say, such is the feasibility and possibility of spirit suggestion, whether one originates or obeys. Inspiration is spirit aid and suggestion, nothing more.

17

Development Through Charity

CHARITY, IN ITS general acceptation, has been identified with alms-giving. Spirit people, with their higher intelligence, contend that charity means giving to those in need our best and purest thought; and they have pointed out that on the earth plane it is rather a mechanical than a spiritual action to distribute material things to others. How many, when they help those in need, give their best thought as well as material aid? True, material assistance is often indispensable; but nevertheless, it should be only a stepping stone to something higher and nobler. A charitable thought, sent out and transmitted by waves of psychic ether, will reach many souls in despair; and, perhaps, lift them to higher conditions in the material as well as in the spirit spheres. There are persons in earth life who are too poor to give material aid, but who, out of the richness of their benevolent hearts, give that which is better, more precious, more Godlike, loving words and kindly deeds.

Such as these are never too tired to offer sympathy, never too weary to speak a cheery word to struggling neighbors. Such persons radiate happiness around them, and are continually sending forth the purest and best of which a soul is capable, and, when they go out into the afterlife, they find that the bread of thought cast upon the waters does return.

It is my custom to ask of spirit people to give some expression of their views on subjects under consideration, and in reply to an inquiry about charity one said:

"And the greatest of all is charity of thought, without which the utmost gifts of money become as pebbles in the mouths of the hungry. Think of all as you would have all think of you. A thought once born grows to its fullness, not only by the good done to the individual, but by its strength and goodness. It circles around, and after encompassing many in its kind embrace, rebounds to enrich the originator. Cultivate the desire to think kindly of your fellow men.

"Some thought dominates all actions. Those who have evil thoughts are in danger of becoming evil themselves, though they may be unconscious of the fact. The mind flings out a radiance which, to some extent, sheds light on every avenue of life. If that radiance should grow feeble and your life selfish, you would long remain in the twilight, and your outlook would be limited. But, if kindness and true charity dominate your thoughts, the radiance will continue rich and bright till its emanations reach the boundaries of hope, and your soul is illumined by the crowning sun of happiness.

"The best way to judge character is to watch the faces of children who turn toward men. A good man loves them and has patience with them, and they turn to him as naturally as a flower follows the warmth of the sun. A bad man realizes their helplessness, and brutally vents his malignity on their small defenseless heads. Such a man is not to be trusted in any walk of life.

"Again be generous to those to whom nature has limited her gifts, for nature compensates, and the time 'will come when all shall be equal. The poorly equipped for earth life will more easily acquire the lessons to be learned in the next, for those of patience and humility are learned already. Those who think differently are to be enlightened, not censured or ridiculed, for all who understand this truth of life's progression are entrusted with the great responsibility of teaching all who can understand; and you must get as close as possible to the lives of others, that your words may have weight.

"Let your hearts be fallow ground, plant therein the seeds of love, charity and purity; nourish them daily with the clear water of tenderness; and you will have a wonderful garden filled with fragrance and white with blossoms, and your life will become a; part of the great life principle.

"A spirit, well known when in earth life, said one evening to a gentleman who worked with me, and who helped obtain the information now given to the public:

"The intense satisfaction that is the constant result of right doing, based on honest purpose, is, in itself, sufficient reward for action. Of all the trite sayings of the Bible, the one that reads, 'What shall it profit a man, if he shall gain the whole world, and yet lose his own soul?' is one with the greatest meaning." Wealth brings many opportunities for good and for evil; in fact, there are more for the latter than for the former, as the besetting sin of mortal man is selfishness and the possession of great riches allows free expression of that greatest of all sources of trouble. The true and full meaning of the word 'selfishness' is in every way opposite to the most beautiful word in your language, 'charity.' Shorn of their meaning, as applied to money, they are the negative and positive of man's character. The fullest opportunity of giving expression to these two opposite words comes with the possession of great wealth. The understanding of the full meaning of these two words is the truest index of a man's character. The ability to make one's life the embodiment of that wonderful word 'charity,' and to understand that other word 'selfishness' so as to avoid it, is the true test of mortal man's ability to control himself.

"Self-control is man's perfect condition. To know charity and practice its meaning; to know selfishness and keep it from you; this is self-control. This state of existence is as near perfection as the earth tied mortal can hope to get. You have been chosen one among many on your side of life to bring certain great truths to the people of the world. In advance of time, you are to be prepared for the time of your usefulness, and this is one of the moments of laying before you certain truths. To teach the truth, the teacher must be truthful; to induce others to accept pure and honest principles, the teacher must be pure and honest himself; to set certain facts before others, the teacher must be above criticism.

"You may honestly atone for those things that have so far occurred in your life, by making amends to those to whom you are indebted. So far as the errors of your past life are concerned, you have well and strongly conquered their chief cause, and you need no longer fear them. You have henceforth no excuse to do otherwise than follow the honorable and ennobling instincts of your nature. Guard well your actions, that they may not be open to criticism from others; and particularly from the one of all others from whom you cannot

escape, your own self. You have been, and you are being, weighed in the balance; and so much is expected
of you, that you must not be found wanting.

"Remember that wealth brings the opportunity to
give expression to what is best in your nature, and that
you will find the only reward for doing good in that intense feeling of satisfaction that can come only as the
result of a good deed, unselfishly done. It is well that
man should earn his daily bread. It is the intention of
nature that every mortal should struggle, for by no other means can he progress in the scale of being. This being so, one so situated that he can live without a proper
exertion on his part, is unfortunate. Never forget this
principle; the waste of money is not charity, but fool-
ishness. You will find many practical ways to do good
and to do it in the right way. A clean tenant demands a
clean habitation. A pure heart and a pure mind are the
results of your own efforts so to keep them.

"Charity is not a formula; it is thought, clothed with
a kind act. Cultivate charity in judging others; try to
draw out the latent good in them, rather than to discover the hidden evil. We must do this if we would rise
to the full glory of our privilege, to the dignity of true
living, to the supreme charity of the world."

18

Fragments

NOTWITHSTANDING THE many years of this research, we were always careful to utilize our strength to the best possible advantage. Little time was spent with tests and personalities, none with frivolities. It was a dignified, scientific work, wherein we sought knowledge to the utmost.

At times there would come concrete and definite statements with great rapidity and of tremendous import. It seemed as if the group of spirit people wanted to say as much as possible in the fewest words. Frequently I asked slower speech, so that my stenographer might get the statements correctly, and I recall being told:

"That it was impossible at times to slow the message; when conditions were right they had to send them through or lose the opportunity."

I have gathered from my records, short terse statements from various communications received from those in the afterlife, some beyond worldly teaching that seem worthy of publication. The following are but a few of thousands; mere fragments of spirit philosophy.

"Force wherever found or how expressed, is life."

"Each change in spirit existence is partly hidden from the plane below, because the conditions of each change make it best for the soul to fit itself for progression without absolute knowledge of the next step."

"When the intellect ceases to be enslaved, the body

becomes free."

"The supreme need of each man is to reason and to remain, ever after, true to his convictions. Where reason leads, each should follow publicly and openly. This is the highest conception of duty."

"Man's conscience is his judgment seat, and reparation for wrong cannot begin too soon. Love for humanity is the basis upon which mankind must stand to gain ultimate good. Brood well upon that with which you store your mind. Each grain of knowledge will grow and bear its fruit."

"Dissolution is simply the throwing aside of the physical garment, the outer covering composed of flesh compounds, whereupon the individual becomes an inhabitant of another sphere of usefulness, differing only in its intensity:"

"Inhabitants of this material world cannot see the spirit form while in the body; neither can they see it when separated from the body."

"All life has intelligence; all intelligence has language; all language, expression."

"One who does right and has the courage of his convictions, will find in the afterlife a radiant happiness, and the censure of this little world will fail to sting."

"A thought born in your mind is for good or evil, a thing to be reckoned with again in the afterlife, when it will confront you face to face, and claim you as its author."

"Do you not think that the great intelligence that planned millions of worlds, and made them move with perfect harmony and precision, that peopled them, that fixed and marked each one's course, and lighted its pathway in infinite space, knows what is best?"

"At dissolution, each sense is quickened, and all that fills space is visible to the spiritual senses and tangible to spiritual touch and brain. Space must then take form, substance and reality – a world of thought, boundless and endless."

"The rains will come when they are timed. They will replenish the green of the harvest and make it richer. The storms of life may beat upon you, but you will find they only break down the dead branches, and you will be more straight and fair for their passing."

"All about this material world there exists actually the psychic or spiritual universe, more active and real than this, peopled with all the countless dead, who, no longer burdened with a physical body, move at will within the boundaries of their sphere, in what appears as space to mortal man."

"In the kingdom of the mind there can be no personal dictation; there is no God but universal good; no Savior but oneself; no trinity but matter, force and mind."

"Life beyond the grave is the promise that hope has ever whispered to all who have lived."

"The sovereignty of the individual must be gained by effort. The weak must be taught; the strongest at some time must bend and obey."

"To every mortal who thinks rightly, Nature's laws become natural laws."

"Dissolution is a step in evolution, and involves no mental change, adding nothing, subtracting nothing, but simply increasing the opportunities for observation and learning."

"Men who deny to others the right of public speech are not qualified for speech themselves."

"If you would impress your thought on others, and spread the truth, make that thought the highest expression of truth."

"Make yourself attuned to the most harmonious vibrations, so that your impulses will be good, and then obey them. They are apt to be the suggestions of a fellow soul working out his salvation."

"Mind is the aggregate of all thoughts. Mind is the universal thought. As a drop of water signifies but one infinitesimal part of the great ocean, so a thought is but one infinitesimal part of the great ocean of mind."

"Deeds are thoughts grown to maturity, and yet a thought unspoken or unlived, will exist through all the ages, as though expressed."

"Everything is governed by law; nothing happens by chance; cause and effect are as potent in the spirit plane as in the earth plane."

"There are sounds that our ears have never heard; there is light that our physical eyes can never see; there is an invisible world filled with people that few have ever imagined."

"Life would be but a futile thing, and all effort useless, if the future did not stretch before us, endless and unlimited in its possibilities."

"The justice that meets the naked soul, on the threshold of its spirit life, is terrible in its completeness."

"The tendency of all life, wheresoever found or howsoever clothed, is to perfect, improve, increase and extend its sphere of usefulness. This is evolution. It is a fact, a law and not a theory, and its possibilities are as boundless as the imagination."

"The atom, alone, has eternal duration of form, for it alone has the power to enter and dominate all other forms. It has no master except force, and to force alone is it amenable."

"The wealth that all in this physical world should seek, has not the ring of gold; it is gathered by right living and by helping others to live right."

"It is far better to have committed an honest error and reaped no profit, than to have great profit and to have honesty gone from your own heart."

"Selfishness in the human heart is the cause of all evil; where selfishness dwells, love can not abide. Selfishness and love can not occupy the same place at the same time."

"An atom from the great ocean of spirit finds lodgment in a physical organism and behold, a man!"

"Mortal needs spirit suggestion, but spirits indeed of mortal thought have just as great a need."

"Life enough is given to rule each day in our kingdom, but not enough for tomorrow."

"Wisdom is born in the soul of man when he recognizes that natural law governs and accounts for all things."

"If a man is clean, he feels clean, and keeping clean inspires him to clean deeds."

"Wisdom, power, beneficence, and the peace that passeth all understanding – these come not from above, but from within."

"If a man can make himself habitually right in his thought and desire, right in his will and purpose, he must become right in the tissues built up out of the mind's action."

"Power is born of desire; no man can earnestly desire to live upon a high plane and yet be compelled to live upon a low plane, since we live in that state of development that we create for ourselves."

"Every life is placed exactly where it should be, and is in touch with the environment needed at that hour to unfold itself."

"It is thought that builds the body. Thought is food, thought is force – the motor power, by means of which the soul expresses itself in physical form."

19

Intellectual Progress

A T THE FUNERAL OF John G. Mills on April 15, 1883, Robert G. Ingersoll, the great agnostic said:" Again we stand face to face with the great mystery that shrouds the world. We question, but there is no reply. Out on the wide waste seas, there drifts no spar. Over the desert of death the Sphinx gazes forever, but does not speak. All wish for happiness beyond this life, all hope to meet again the loved and lost. Immortality is a word that Hope through all the ages has been whispering to Love. The mystery of life and death, we cannot understand. The golden bridge of life from gloom emerges, and on shadow rests. Beyond this we do not know. Fate is speechless, destiny is dumb, and the secret of the future has never yet been told. We love, we wait, we hope.

"What can we say of death? What can we say of the dead? Where they have gone, reason cannot go, and from thence revelation has not come.

"This is a fair statement by a fair man of the general understanding of that subject at that time.

Since those words were uttered, more progress has been made than in the thousand years prior to that time. The telephone has come into practical use, the automobile has displaced the horse, electricity lights the world and propels our engines and cars. The human voice is heard across the continent and over the ocean. We navigate the air, and ships call to each other over the waters for help when in distress. Progress has not been confined to things physical. Within that time we have also come to know what that change called death is, and are able to comprehend the process involved and to explain it scientifically. Its mystery, like all other mysteries, disappears when the simple natural law is understood. Earnest men have called and questioned, the dead have answered, and life and death is, in a measure, understood. We find there is no golden bridge, no dark stream, to cross; all life is one on different planes.

Where the so-called dead have gone, reason has now followed, and the revelation has come from those who live and labor beyond our vision and touch. We now know what physical change takes place at the time of dissolution, and, when conditions are properly met, we now may talk with those who seem to have left us, voice to voice.

This is not the discovery of any one man. For the last decade and more, great thinkers have devoted their thought and energy to discover what before was a mystery, and have had the courage to give the world the result of their scientific investigations. More has been written on this subject in the last twenty years than on perhaps any other, but only a small percentage of those classed as thinkers know it – only those who think for themselves read this class of literature. The great majority never give this subject a thought and do not want to know, though it is of more vital importance than any other matter. Some there are who face the east and sincerely welcome the light; others stand with their backs to the sunrise and worship the sunset of the day before.

Among well known scholars who stand for this

great truth may be mentioned Wallace, Crookes, Rear-Admiral Moore, Stead, Lodge and Doyle, of England; Richet, of France; Lombroso, of Italy; Stanford, of Australia; Wu Ting Tang, of China; Carrington, Funk and Professor Hyslop, of America. All these have written on their individual discoveries, based on evidential facts. This field has been fully covered. The continuity of life has been proved and as well established as any other fact in nature. But these facts and incidents are so out of the ordinary that the human mind has difficulty in grasping them. It is difficult to comprehend what one has not actually experienced.

I do not intend to make this presentation technically evidential, except as the incidents related and the source of my knowledge carry conviction. I want to come to the public through the valley of reason, so to present my facts that they appeal to all, for when they are found reasonable and in accordance with nature's law and purpose, they will be accepted. They must be accepted, for the facts have been gathered from those who are now in the afterlife; and who can better describe what death, so-called, is than those who have passed through it? Who can better explain the conditions under which they live, and the place, than men of earth who now live there?

I was able to do this work, because of the assistance of Emily S. French, then the world's finest voice psychic, who gave the latter years of her life to this work and to me, without money and without price. She was so deaf that she seldom heard the spirit voices, and during the latter years frail and blind; but in her presence the dead spoke, and all within sound of spirit voices could hear as well as I could, and hundreds at my invitation did so.

Interest in this subject has grown tremendously of late years. There are circles of investigators in almost every town and city, as well as in many private homes. In this manner the work is carried forward. It has been my privilege to talk with Ingersoll, from whose speech I have quoted, on many occasions. I have heard his spirit voice ring with the volume of his earlier years. His eloquence no man ever equaled. He established identity and told of his work in the afterlife, as well as of his mission in this, which was to arouse and make people think. He is doing the same work now, only with greater understanding, and, because of this privilege and because of his answer to the doubts he expressed, I quote from his speech. He has answered all the questions he asked when here, and in these chapters, though I seldom use names, are various statements made by him as to conditions which he finds in that life.

With all my research and opportunity, I have come to know just a little of the conditions in and along the Frontier. Ages will be required to come into full knowledge. Nature puts before our eyes more than we can see, in our ears more than we can hear, and to the mind more than it: can comprehend. We gather what we sow, gain what we work for, and have no right to expect something for nothing. We cannot get knowledge without study, understanding without thinking, but right thinking slowly and surely brings knowledge. What I hope to do is to set in motion a line of reasoning, based on the facts that I have stated, which will appeal to all who read this work, and through such process and original research, lead to understanding. Then shall we do those things that will enrich beyond the grave, and enable one to enter the new life with dignity and credit. In view of the progress in knowledge that has been made in this field, it is not unreasonable for me to hope to do this. The thinking mind should not require proof of survival.

We know nothing can be destroyed, as nothing in nature ever has been. The idea that man can be annihilated, when a clod of earth cannot be, is preposterous. The thinker should start with the proposition that man survives, and then bend his efforts to know in what invisible plane he functions. It is really not a question of whether life continues, but where and how. Darwin, foremost among naturalists, Wagner, the greatest of composers, Hugo, poet and patriot, Huxley and Faraday, among the scientists, Chopin, Mendelssohn, Mozart, Beethoven, Paganini, Verdi and Liszt, among the musicians, Gladstone, Lincoln and Roosevelt, the world's great statesmen, are not dead. These mighty rivers of intellectual thought and beauty have not ceased to flow, for in death they reach the sea. In other fields of opportunity these great minds labor on – such individualities can never die; this earth life but prepared them for a greater work. How absurd, too, for one to think that the Master Intelligence, working through nature would produce such great souls and then, just in the fullness of their mentality, destroy them.

It seems almost presumption for me to undertake to prove continuity, so certain to the thinking mind.

The only justification I can find is in the fact that this whole subject has been given little consideration by the many and is, therefore, little known. In making this presentation, I recognize no distinction among men. It is equally important that the non-thinker should understand what earth life leads to, as it is for the intellectual. In the democracy of death, only spirituality counts. When we look up into the sky, and see nothing between us and the stars, we are really looking through a realm as rich in detail as the landscape we can see on a fine day from a mountain top. This region is inhabited by myriads of the human family, among them many we have loved and lost and will rejoin in due time. And this is not guesswork nor metaphysical speculation but the definite result of observation, as scientific in character as that concerned with astronomy or spectroscopic analysis.

20

Looking Into the Future

"THE BOOK IS MADE." At a dinner given by the Buffalo Bar Association, these words fell from the lips of its guest of honor, one of the most distinguished lawyers in America. It was a notable gathering. He had returned from a larger field of endeavor, rich in worldly goods. His career had been remarkable. In the fullness of his success, with a record of seventy years behind him, he had come back for a day to meet those whom he knew in other times.

This man, generous to a fault, friendly in manner, ever ready to serve the public good, candid and masterful in speech, a great citizen, intellectually honest, thoroughly informed in worldly affairs, but without a particle of knowledge beyond this world of men, having all the glory that could come from professional life, seeing nothing beyond, sadly said, to that eager group that came to do him honor, "The Book is made."

This great mind, engrossed in the affairs of the present, like the great majority of mankind, had not had time to inquire, much less to learn, what this life leads to.

Knowing nothing of a future, he felt his life work was finished. It was December; the sun was so low that the shadows fell in front, and his thoughts went back in memory to dreams of youth. Had he known that all his years of labor but prepared him for a life of more intense reality, following upon the heels of this, he would have said:

"The foreword has been written, and in the great beyond I will write the book in acts and kindly deeds.

"We, who have come in touch with life in the great beyond, look with a sorrow that words cannot express upon those who neither know nor care; and those who fear what they call death we would lead from darkness into light and knowledge. Why should we fear that which has or will come to all, in accordance with nature's law? We cannot tell which is the greater blessing, birth or dissolution; both are good. It has been a great privilege to have had birth and growth and love, with all the joy that has been ours. All has been in accordance with nature, and nature is God. But the end comes not with that natural change so long called death, which we know to be according to nature. Even if we did not actually know what followed, any thinking mind should appreciate that all changes in nature are for our good. Over every cradle Nature bends and smiles, and tenderly to those whom we think dead she beckons and welcomes. For into this zone we pass bodily, our inner body the same as now, holding all the failures and triumphs met with in this journey. Those conditions no honest man should fear.

The idea of immortality, like the sea, has ebbed and flowed in the human heart, beating with endless waves, since time began. All hope that they may reach the shore, but the words hope and faith concede that the fact is unknown. Uncertainty and ignorance breed fear. If one must rest his salvation on belief alone, let it be the gospel of help; a kind act is better than a theory.

This life is designed to fit us for a greater work. I do not criticize Nature, or the Master Intelligence that planned our progression. I have not arrived at the state of mind where I feel competent to criticize any natural law. All others are conceded for our good. Why not the last? And if that be true, why weep and shed bitter tears, when in this change we advance to another and higher existence?

The microscope discovered a new world, the telescope millions more. Everywhere has been found infinite life. In all explorations there has been found nothing independent of, or superior to, Nature, and in that presence I find God.

Common notions about death are all wrong. Nothing ever dies. None who have gone ever want to come back. Must not that life be most engaging and fair? When a good man goes, his soul is filled with light, for his good deeds shine like stars. A noble life enriches itself and all the world. But all lives are not lived worthily. Think of the vast multitude, the endless procession, that hourly pass, leaving no thought, no truth, as a legacy of mankind.

From the frontiers of the afterlife, from that belt or zone where spirit people live, they send us cheering messages, they speak in full toned voice and write, as when they lived among us. And so we come to know the dead have never died.

And then again we are told, that in the next plane, the continuation of this, the basest soul will find its way and have the everlasting chance of doing right, and that the better souls, the finer men and women, pass at once to opportunity and happiness.

In these chapters I have stated facts and narrated incidents as I have come to know them from those actually living in the afterlife. With all the strength that

I possess, with all the personality that lies behind a life of effort, I vouch for the truth of what I have written. I sought in the beginning to bring to the understanding propositions of vital importance, though practically new to every thinking mind. I restate them as follows:

Here and now, within our physical and visible bodies, is an invisible, living, active, inner body, composed and made up of substance or material which we term ether; it is this body that is permanent, holding form, feature and expression, while the outer flesh covering, with which it is clothed, changes from hour to hour; death or dissolution is but the final separation of the inner body, which is invisible before as well as after, from the physical body. The spirit body passes into the next etheric plane of existence, vibrating in harmony with all that is there, where all is just as tangible and material to them as this plane is to us who are still in the physical. This change is Nature's process for advancing our plane of activity, and is not to be feared any more than birth.

The next fact that I would bring to human consciousness is the location of this afterlife, where spirit people live. No subject is so little known and so vital to our understanding. Let me restate this condition as follows:

Around and about the earth are belts or zones of exceeding fine matter, a substance called ether, varying in character or density, very similar to those belts or zones that the telescope has discovered about the planets Jupiter and Saturn. They are all just as much substance as the earth itself, the outer belts or zones being higher in vibration and lighter than those that touch and really blend with the earth itself. In those zones, from the substance that composes them, all structures and things are built and formed naturally, as here. They have fields and meadow land, rugged mountains and deep forests, homes, buildings, books, paintings, music, sculpture and institutions of learning. What we have are imperfect imitations of what exists, and first existed, there.

Too long we have held the thought that the universe was specially created for us. The infinite mind which formed and fashioned this planet, who fixed its pathways and made the definite law through which mankind should obtain his development, had the wisdom, power and intelligence to create and provide conditions and a place in nature for man to finish what was here begun. Because we have not heretofore discovered and located the boundaries of the next life, should not lead us to the conclusion that such place or condition has not existed from the beginning. Men did not know of the continent of America until 1492, but it had been here millions of years before. We have not had actual knowledge of the afterlife until of late, but it too has existed for all time.

If this book serves the purpose for which it is designed, it will bring to the consciousness of those who reason the two propositions, if nothing more.

Visualizing the future, I see the churches that have not kept pace in the march of progress, opening their doors to the demonstration and proof of what they teach. I see the abandonment of creeds and faith and all beliefs, knowledge taking their place, and ministers aiding psychic research. I see a world coming to understand the inexorable laws of nature, and realizing that the only wealth worthy of effort comes from helping others and adding to the happiness of mankind, understanding that by such acts we spiritualize, refine and enrich the soul, and clothe the inner body with a garment woven from the fabric of love and generous deeds. I see psychic investigation reduced to a greater science commanding the attention of our best minds. This field of exploration transcends all that have been discovered, and its possibilities are unlimited. I see selfishness and greed lessen, as we come to know that for every act of oppression and advantage we in the end must pay the price, for the laws of nature require exact compensation. I see the coming of the time when one who is called upon to act will inquire of himself, "Is it just and fair?"

Looking again, I see a world of people living nobler and finer lives, helped by the teaching of their spirit kinsmen, who bring home to human consciousness the necessity of living this life according to our ideals if we would not go poor into the afterlife of opportunity.

I see fear of dissolution gone from the human heart, understanding taking its place, as we appreciate that in dissolution the Master Intelligence has planned a method, like birth, by which we may take a step in our eternal progression.

In the last analysis, there comes to each the question of where, at the journey's end, he will find himself. Many never permit themselves to think about it, hoping, possibly, by so doing, that they may escape something, ignoring the fact that earth life is designed to fit us for that most important event, and that each is accountable for the opportunities that have been his.

This is a matter of scientific fact. Faith will not take the place of acts, beliefs will not help, confession will not change conditions that a lifetime has made, for it will take as long to change what we have created for ourselves as it did to build.

Dissolution will not add to or subtract from the conditions we have made. If we have been criminal or debased, the great law of attraction will draw us with those of similar character, separate and apart from others. If we have lived immoral lives, we shall find ourselves herded among those of like kind. If we have been idle and have not improved our minds, we shall find ourselves among the indolent. If we have been selfish, then we will be in the dark, with only selfish companions, for the only light one carries, radiates from his own etheric body. If we have lived cleanly and fairly, been charitable and helpful to those less fortunate than we, and have done right according to our understanding, our souls become spiritualized; they will radiate light, by which we may see he glories of the afterlife as we enter into the fullness thereof. Nature metes out exact justice to everyone. We inherit what we have created, and nothing more.

I see good in every act of kindness, in all the words of tenderness that fall from human lips, and to me the sum of all the good in all the world is God.

Also available from
White Crow Books

Marcus Aurelius—*The Meditations*
ISBN 978-1-907355-20-2

Elsa Barker—*Letters from a Living Dead Man*
ISBN 978-1-907355-83-7

Elsa Barker—*War Letters from the Living Dead Man*
ISBN 978-1-907355-85-1

Elsa Barker—*Last Letters from the Living Dead Man*
ISBN 978-1-907355-87-5

Richard Maurice Bucke—*Cosmic Consciousness*
ISBN 978-1-907355-10-3

G. K. Chesterton—*The Everlasting Man*
ISBN 978-1-907355-03-5

G. K. Chesterton—*Heretics*
ISBN 978-1-907355-02-8

G. K. Chesterton—*Orthodoxy*
ISBN 978-1-907355-01-1

Arthur Conan Doyle—*The Edge of the Unknown*
ISBN 978-1-907355-14-1

Arthur Conan Doyle—*The New Revelation*
ISBN 978-1-907355-12-7

Arthur Conan Doyle—*The Vital Message*
ISBN 978-1-907355-13-4

Arthur Conan Doyle with Simon Parke—*Conversations with Arthur Conan Doyle*
ISBN 978-1-907355-80-6

Leon Denis with Arthur Conan Doyle—*The Mystery of Joan of Arc*
ISBN 978-1-907355-17-2

The Earl of Dunraven—*Experiences in Spiritualism with D. D. Home*
ISBN 978-1-907355-93-6

Meister Eckhart with Simon Parke—*Conversations with Meister Eckhart*
ISBN 978-1-907355-18-9

Kahlil Gibran—*The Forerunner*
ISBN 978-1-907355-06-6

Kahlil Gibran—*The Madman*
ISBN 978-1-907355-05-9

Kahlil Gibran—*The Prophet*
ISBN 978-1-907355-04-2

Kahlil Gibran—*Sand and Foam*
ISBN 978-1-907355-07-3

Kahlil Gibran—*Jesus the Son of Man*
ISBN 978-1-907355-08-0

Kahlil Gibran—*Spiritual World*
ISBN 978-1-907355-09-7

Hermann Hesse—*Siddhartha*
ISBN 978-1-907355-31-8

D. D. Home—*Incidents in my Life Part 1*
ISBN 978-1-907355-15-8

Mme. Dunglas Home; edited, with an Introduction, by Sir Arthur Conan Doyle—*D. D. Home: His Life and Mission*
ISBN 978-1-907355-16-5

Allan Kardec—*The Spirits Book*
ISBN 978-1-907355-98-1

Lucius Annaeus Seneca—*On Benefits*
ISBN 978-1-907355-19-6

Rebecca Ruter Springer—*Intra Muros—My Dream of Heaven*
ISBN 978-1-907355-11-0

W. T. Stead—*After Death* or *Letters from Julia: A Personal Narrative*
ISBN 978-1-907355-89-9

Leo Tolstoy, edited by Simon Parke—*Tolstoy's Forbidden Words*
ISBN 978-1-907355-00-4

Leo Tolstoy—*A Confession*
ISBN 978-1-907355-24-0

Leo Tolstoy—*The Gospel in Brief*
ISBN 978-1-907355-22-6

Leo Tolstoy—*The Kingdom of God is Within You*
ISBN 978-1-907355-27-1

Leo Tolstoy—*My Religion: What I Believe*
ISBN 978-1-907355-23-3

Leo Tolstoy—*On Life*
ISBN 978-1-907355-91-2

Leo Tolstoy—*Twenty-three Tales*
ISBN 978-1-907355-29-5

Leo Tolstoy—*What is Religion and other writings*
ISBN 978-1-907355-28-8

Leo Tolstoy—*Work While Ye Have the Light*
ISBN 978-1-907355-26-4

Leo Tolstoy with Simon Parke—*Conversations with Tolstoy*
ISBN 978-1-907355-25-7

Vincent Van Gogh with Simon Parke—*Conversations with Van Gogh*
ISBN 978-1-907355-950

Howard Williams with an Introduction by Leo Tolstoy—*The Ethics of Diet: An Anthology of Vegetarian Thought*
ISBN 978-1-907355-21-9

All titles available as eBooks, and select titles available in Audiobook format from www.whitecrowbooks.com

CPSIA information can be obtained
at www.ICGtesting.com
Printed in the USA
BVHW081332310321
603805BV00008B/1025